ASPECTS OF PILTON'S HISTORY

Produced for The Pilton Village History Group

Reprinted November 2011.

Printed by Emprint , Dyehouse Lane, Glastonbury

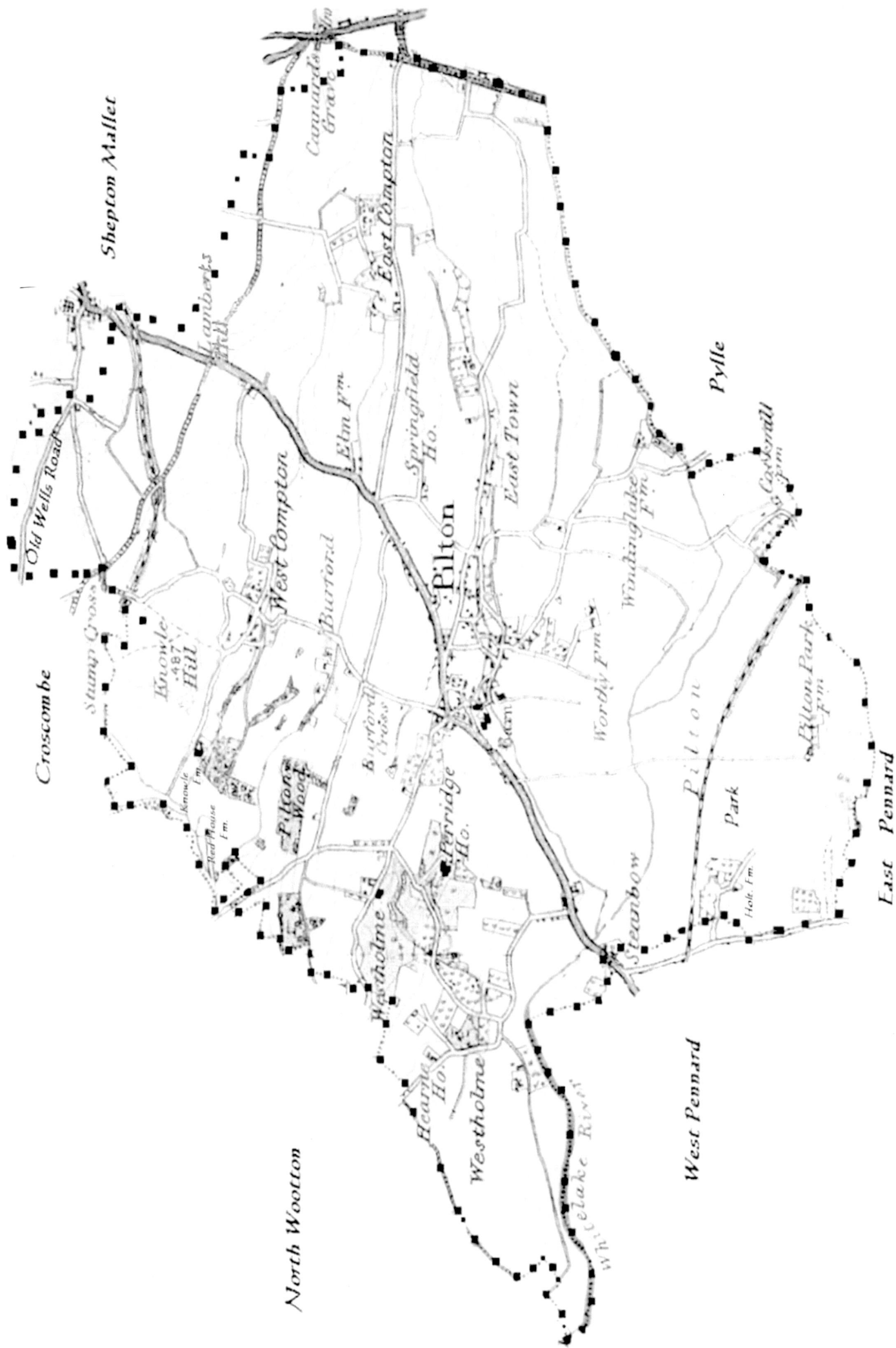

Shepton Mallet

Croscombe

North Wootton

West Pennard

East Pennard

Pylle

Old Wells Road

Lambert's Hill

East Compton

Springfield Ho.

East Town

Pilton

West Compton

Burford

Stump Cross

Knowle 487 Hill

Knowle Fm

Pilton Wood

Red House Fm

Burford House

Ferridge Ho.

Westholme

Hearnes Ho.

Westholme

Whitelake River

Steanbow

Pilton Park

Park

Holt Fm

Pilton Park Fm

Cockmill Fm

Windmylake Fm

Worthy Fm

Elm Fm

PREFACE

Welcome to "Aspects Of Pilton's History ". The book is divided into sections which are more or less arranged chronologically , but as each section stands by itself they can be profitably read in any order. Indeed many may wish to start with the last section (section 15) which covers places in Pilton Village which will be familiar , leaving the less familiar topics to be delved into when the inclination and time arise. In addition to being a history, the book serves as a reference book .To this end an extensive appendix covers the sources available about Pilton, and where to go for more information. The appendix also includes much additional detail on some topics .

As the title suggests only some of Pilton's History is chronicled in this book, and in particular very little of the 20th. century is covered. This leaves plenty of areas that could be usefully explored in the future. Even within those topics that are covered I am very conscious of the number of times that lack of information has resulted in "maybe" and "possibly" when more research could give us some certainties. It is hoped therefore that the book will help to stimulate further research.

It is anticipated that most readers will have local knowledge of Pilton, but for those who haven't , a map of the Parish is included . The Parish is roughly 5 miles from east to west, and 4 from north to south, with the village centre situated 2-3 miles south west of the centre of Shepton Mallet. Its land area is nearly 5,000 acres which makes it one of the larger Civil Parishes in Somerset .The 2001 census gives Pilton's population as 935 from 381 households.

Acknowledgments: I would like to express my thanks to all those who gave me encouragement to write this book, and to the many people who have in the past loaned photographs and provided information to the Pilton Village History Group. In particular two of the ex- chairmen of the History Group: Ken Dilkes for starting the first re-draft of "The Walk Around Pilton," and Richard Rainsford for his painstaking proof reading, his useful comments, and his enthusiastic encouragement, also my thanks to the present chairman John Fletcher for his moral support and proof reading skills.

Finally, this book is dedicated to David Chapman, who died after illness in March this year. Dave was a keen and active member of The History Group for many years and his presence is much missed.

Keith Harlow.

Nov. 2008

================CONTENTS================

SECTION 1

===============BEGINNINGS===============

Origins

When in search of origins there are a number of questions which seem naturally to surface. For example, how far back in time can one go? When did it all start? What was there before? Who first set foot in the area? Such questions and others like them can seldom be completely answered as the necessary information and archaeological evidence is simply unavailable. Nevertheless by drawing on knowledge of nearby areas, some broad indications about Pilton can be drawn.

Around 200 million years ago most of England was submerged under water. In particular, what was to become central Somerset formed a warm shallow sea. For many millions of years sea life lived, died, and sank to the sea floor. It is upon this cemetery of sea creatures that limestone is formed. Eventually the sea receded leaving behind Liassic beds which have contributed much to Pilton's architectural heritage. At first soft and muddy, the beds hardened and compressed in time to form the characteristic limestone of the area, Blue Lias. Virtually all the old buildings of Pilton are built with this attractive stone, and

it is still quarried in Pilton on an occasional basis. Amongst the more recent buildings using this local stone are the residences at John Burns Cottages, and amongst the oldest is the Church.

Early Man

The earliest record of human habitation in Somerset and indeed in all Europe lies not too far from Pilton in limestone caves above Westbury –sub- Mendip. Finds there have been dated to as far back as ½ million years and include bone and some flint fragments suggestive of an early presence of man.

Coming closer to the present, on a path leading to Wookey Hole Caves, archaeological remains have been uncovered in a cave [known as Hyena Den] suggesting human habitation there around 34,000 years ago. The remains are typical of those associated with the Neanderthals, a species which modern man is thought to have replaced.

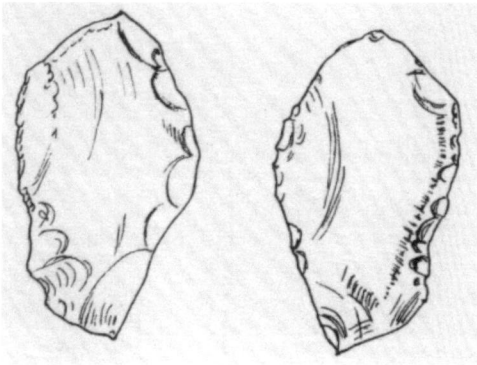

A flint tool possibly more than 8,000 years old found near Barrow House

caves of Cheddar and Wookey around this time. One find at Cheddar was particularly interesting. A skeleton was initially found in 1903 but not analysed in depth until the mid 1990's.It was found to date from c. 7150 B.C.and its DNA matched closely to that of a local history teacher, suggesting a direct descent on his mother's side for over 9000 years. He has come to be known as Cheddar Man ,and would have been a hunter gatherer, living mainly off the deer, wild boar, wolves and bears which inhabited the area at the time.

The existence of Man's presence in the area could not have been continuous as there were cycles of Ice Ages stretching back to half a million years ago and beyond.

The last one covered much of England but its ice sheet didn't come further south than Gloucestershire. Despite Somerset having escaped the more extreme temperatures, it would still have been too cold in Pilton for settled human habitation. The ice started its withdrawal from about 13,000 years B.C. onwards and within a few hundred years temperatures were sufficiently high to encourage migrants to re-enter Britain via the then existing land link with Europe. However there were still extreme temperature fluctuations and later it turned much colder again ,probably too much so for settled human habitation .

Stone Age axe head c 2,400 B.C. found near Mount Pleasant

It is only from about 8,000 B.C. onwards that any continuous human existence in England can be demonstrated. Indeed humans were known to have inhabited the sheltered

Flint arrowhead found near Perridge

By 6.500 B.C. sea levels had risen, England had become an island and Somerset was separated from South Wales by The Severn Estuary. The tundra-like conditions which existed at the end of the Ice Age had given way gradually and by 6,000 years B.C denser deciduous woodland had emerged and established itself throughout most of England. This would also would have been the case in Pilton where soil depths allowed, and more extensive and varied hunting would have been possible.

By this time Southern Europeans had started farming and had learnt how to domesticate some farm animals, but it was not until around 4500 B.C. that migration from the south brought this knowledge to Britain. Up until this time the means of living relied almost entirely on hunting and gathering. There were no natural caves in Pilton to offer a sheltered base such as those in Cheddar, and probably Pilton was only passed through and hunted in rather than settled upon.

Early indications of man's presence in Pilton is from the finding of a flint hand tool just south of the ford near Barrow House in Pilton village. Such tools are difficult to date as they were used by early people for thousands of years. However it is typical of the Old Stone Age and may possibly date back 8,000 years [see illustration on previous page].

Early Farmers

By about 4,000 B.C. farming communities were known to exist in and around the Somerset Levels. Their economy was one of mixed farming, growing cereal crops in forest clearings, keeping animals such as cattle, sheep

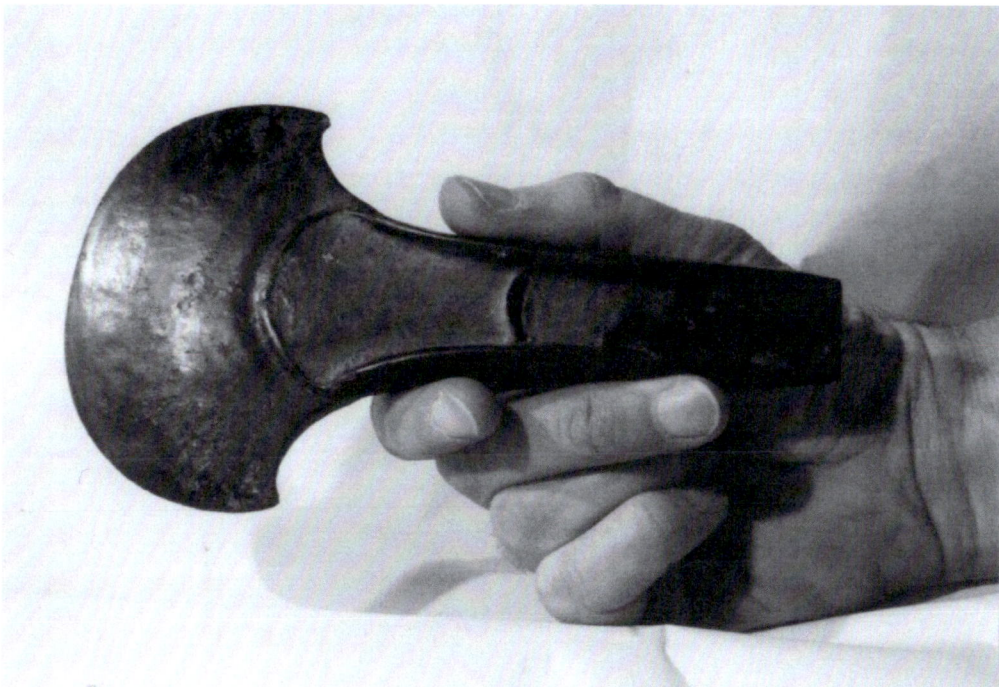

Bronze axe head found at Cumhill Farm

surviving artefacts are flint tools, stone axes and pottery. Some of these people, living in and around the swamplands just north of Glastonbury were sufficiently sophisticated and organised by 3,800 B.C. to have constructed wooden walkways through the swamps extending to a mile or so in length. They split oak trees to make planks and used pegs from hundreds of trees for their walkways, no mean feat using only stone tools to help them . With such well established and settled communities on Pilton's doorstep it is likely that people had soon also settled in Pilton itself. Any estimate of a settlement date must at present be very broad but it is likely to be no more than a couple of centuries after 3,800 B.C at the latest.

Another artefact   left behind in Pilton by early man was a stone age axe possibly 2,400 years old. This was of polished Cornish greenstone and found near Mount Pleasant. Evidence of Bronze Age [2,000 to 650 B.C]   activities includes a very handsome Bronze Axe head dug up 1/3 mile south of the Abbey Barn, and small barbed and tanged flint arrow heads found on the hillside south east of Perridge House, [two almost complete flint arrowheads were found together with other pieces of worked flint and a single piece of the rim of a "pottery bowl" while digging a trench for a gas pipe-line.].

Tribal Somerset

In pre- Roman times England was split between a number of Celtic tribes who had migrated from the low countries of Europe from around 400 B.C. onwards. The tribal territories began to crystallise out around 100 B.C. with most of Northern Somerset belonging to a tribe called the Dobunnii , and another tribe called the Durotriges to the south and east stretching down to the south coast. It is not entirely clear which tribe Pilton was part of as it was on the borders of the two, and in any case exact boundaries are likely to have shifted over time .Most likely however is that Pilton came under The Durotriges tribe. This was a loose confederation of smaller tribes with major bases at Dorchester in Dorset, and later at Ilchester in Somerset.

The normal habitation was an extended family all living together in a large roundhouse with thatched roofs of straw or heather. The walls were probably made from wattle and daub, but in some areas they were of stone. Groups of roundhouses were often close together surrounded by a wooden palisade on top of a stone wall that circuited the whole

A typical large roundhouse

settlement. This gave protection for them and their animals against wilder animals such as wolves and wild boar. Excavations at Cannards Grave just outside the Parish have uncovered the outline of the bases of three of these roundhouses, but as yet none have been discovered in Pilton

SECTION 2

=======ROMANS, SAXONS, NORMANS ========

The Romans

Shortly after the Roman Claudius successfully invaded England in A.D 43 he set about bringing the country under Roman rule. One of the aids to establishing control was to improve communications in the form of better roads. The Fosse Way was an essential part of the Emperor's overall scheme of subjugating England to Roman rule. Constructed around 49A.D, it still defines the east boundary of Pilton Parish. Remains of an extensive Roman settlement have been found to the east side of Shepton Mallet in the Cannards Grave area. No doubt the Pilton farmers would have benefited from selling farm produce to this settlement.

Despite this strong Roman presence on Pilton's door-step there are few signs within Pilton itself that The Romans had been in the area. There has however been one set of discoveries indicating their presence. These were made on the far southern slopes of Pilton (1/4 mile south of Worthy Farmhouse). A number of Romano- British (1st. To 4th. century) pottery shards were uncovered while digging drainage ditches. One piece was identified as Samian Ware, pottery imported from France during Roman times. Some pieces are thick and gritty, others smooth grey and delicate, a few pieces being dark red.

The 400 years of Roman rule left surprisingly little long-term effects on the native inhabitants of England .Yes they left us some good roads but alas no tradition of building them. At the time their Villas were something to behold especially compared with the rustic huts of Stone Age Britain They were however much too grand for the populace and soon decayed and vanished from the land once the Romans had left.

One of the changes the Roman period saw was a wider use of bread wheat, though its rise to dominance was to be a post Roman trend. Otherwise stable crops changed little, with the possible exception of the introduction of 'relish' plants, herbs and spices. There is some evidence of a rise in viticulture and improvements to the plough being used which helped speed up and improve soil cultivation. The water mill was also introduced to England during Roman times .

The Saxons

In 410 A.D. the Romans went back to Rome and left England to look after itself. The Dark ages had begun. At first the lives of the locals probably changed very little as the basis of the English tribal system survived the period of Roman rule. .

Soon however, England disintegrated into various warring groups led by chiefs from both home-grown and foreign invaders. By the 6th.century Saxon raids on England became increasingly regular. The invaders gradually gained the upper hand and various tribes from Northern Germany began to settle. The invaders called themselves 'Engle' or 'Englise' which was Latinised to Anglis. Gradually they drifted westwards conquering local tribes and either assimilating them or driving them further west. The tide of conquest paused and their king became king of the west Saxons to distinguish him from other Saxon groups occupying England at that time. The name was soon abbreviated to Westsexe and hence Wessex. Prior to 658 A.D. there were still large numbers of Britons in the Glastonbury area and although Pilton's position is unknown for certain it was probably still British at that time. There was some decisive fighting in 658 which the British lost and it was probably from around this time that Pilton became firmly Saxon Whether the native British population stayed to become assimilated or were replaced by the Saxons is not known, probably both happened to some extent.

It is probably from around the 7th. century that Pilton's name became established. It is thought to be made up of two Saxon parts, *Pil-* , meaning a stream or creek derived probably from The Saxon *pyl*, and -*tun* meaning a settlement, enclosure or farm- thus 'the settlement by the stream'. Many other local parishes would seem to have been named in Saxon times and this helps to support the idea of the Pilton name originating at the time of, or shortly after the Saxon invasion of this part of Somerset. In Pilton itself the Saxons left little evidence of their existence and only one piece of Saxon pottery has been found.

Anglo Saxon Charters

From AD 674-726 King Ine was ruler of Wessex, and it was this King who was said to have granted Pilton to the Benedictine monks at Glastonbury .They possessed charters dated 705 A.D., supposedly from King Ine proving this grant. Although this may have been so, the charters and documents supporting the grant are considered by historians who have studied them to be somewhat dodgy. At best they contain elements of fiction and at worse may be complete make believe, with no one knowing for certain what was fact and what was fiction. The constructing of charters to justify title to land was a popular pastime of the monks and indeed at times essential for them in order to 'prove' possession if their originals had been lost or destroyed.

Nevertheless King Ine was generally known to have endowed a number of religious houses with land and much to Glastonbury in particular. He was a devoutly religious man and even gave up his Kingship in order to make a pilgrimage to Rome. Only someone of great standing and wealth would have been able to give away such a large area as Pilton, and the Benedict monks were not known to have been in the habit of stealing other people's land. Neither are there any other nobles or kings who are recorded to have granted Pilton.There are strong indications therefore that at least the essence of the grant is based in reality and if so the balance of probability is that Pilton was indeed in the hands of Glastonbury Abbey as early as 705.

However Glastonbury's rule over Pilton may not have remained for long, as the Viking raids in later centuries are thought to have caused Glastonbury to lose control over most of its lands. Indeed, the Monastery itself probably ceased to exist for a short while. William of Malmesbury, a respected Monk historian was commissioned in the 12th century by Glastonbury to write its history. He concluded that there had been no monks there from the time of King Alfred until the early-10th. century. Later, the lands were claimed back and by the 11th. century Glastonbury and Pilton was firmly back in the Monastery's hands.

Domesday

Ipsa æccla ten PILTONE. T.R.E. geldb p. xx. hid. Tra. e̅
xxx. car̅. Pter hanc h̅ abb ibi tram. xx. car̅. quæ nunq̨
geldau̅. In d̅nio s̅t. x. car̅. 7 xv. serui. 7 xxi. uills 7 XLII.
bord cu̅. x. car̅ sup tra̅ n̅ geldant. Ibi. II. molini redd

The first 4 lines of the Pilton entry in the Domesday book-see appendix for the translation

Twenty years after the Norman William the Conqueror had subdued England, he commissioned a survey of the country to assess the value of his property. Its aim was to find out just how much tax he should be getting, and whether more could be obtained. This survey, known as the Domesday Book, was nation wide and gives us details of 34 counties and 9,250 manors. It was completed in 1086 and provides the first reliable documentation about Pilton. The south west is fortunate as two versions of the survey have survived and thus gives us more information than is generally available in some other areas; both have been used in this summary.

The survey shows us that the Manor of Pilton was held by Glastonbury Abbey. Prior to 1066 Pilton was shown as a very much larger area than now as it also encompassed the sub areas

of Shepton, Croscombe, Wootton and Pylle. Probably in the pre-conquest era Pilton with its sub areas were managed as one very large estate with Pilton at its centre. (The historian Michael Costen believed the estate to date back to Celtic times with its origins in the Romano-British period.)

However William wanted fighting men, and in order to provide them Glastonbury leased out Shepton, Croscombe, and Pylle to help provide the necessary armoured Knights [Knight Fees.]. Although the Glastonbury Abbots remained the Overlord of these sub- areas they thereafter effectively lost control of their destinies and they developed their own separate histories. Pilton on the other hand continued to be directly controlled by Glastonbury and its Abbots for another 500 or so years. North Wootton at the time of Domesday was leased to a Monk but had returned to Glastonbury's direct control within a few years. In latter centuries its affairs became intermingled with Pilton's much more so than any of the other surrounding areas.

The Domesday Book was so called as it was considered a book of reckoning and there was no escaping it.

As far as we can tell the Domesday boundary of Pilton was much the same as the modern Parish but with two notable exceptions.

Firstly, a small area in pre- conquest Pilton (squashed between Croscombe and Shepton Mallet) was retained in post conquest Pilton. It was a detached area of 460 acres known as

Ham and completely surrounded by these two Manors. .It remained part of Pilton until the local government reforms of the 1890's,when it was divided between Croscombe and Shepton Mallet. Just why the monks set up this arrangement is unclear, but it is probably

usually reckoned that these were only the heads of households and did not include the rest of the family. A multiplier of 4 to 5 is therefore used to obtain a measure of the total

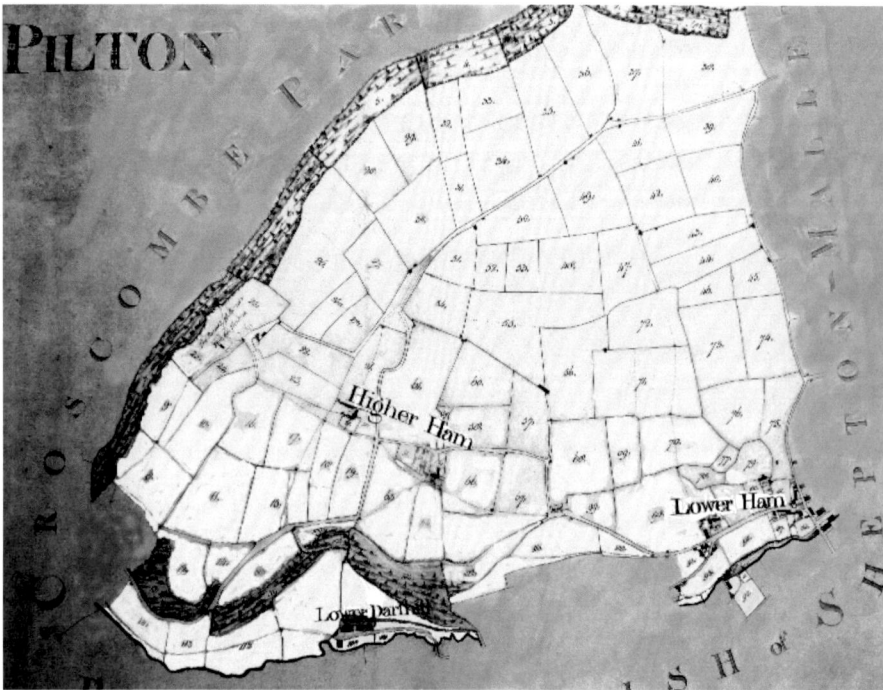

An 1809 map of Ham. The main part of Pilton is to the south. The river at the bottom of the picture is The river Sheppey west of Shepton Mallet, and forms much of Ham's southern border.

related to the fact that Ham had excellent resources of woodland, and that the river Sheppey (which ran along the southern edge of Ham) was more suitable and reliable for driving a mill than any other stream in Pilton. The Monks may well have wanted to keep direct control of these rare resources.

The second exception is that after 1066 a segment of Pilton was given to another Manor as part of a Knight's Fee. The amount of land involved was not large, probably in the region of 240 to 360 acres, [Domesday lists it as having only 1 smallholder, 1 slave and 1 plough] but it would have been entirely outside the control and administration of the rest of Pilton. It is thought that the area was based around Perridge House (but see section 8 for more information).

Domesday lists the residents of Pilton as 15 slaves, 21 villagers and 42 smallholders. It is

population. This gives us an estimate of 312 to 390 as Pilton's population at that time. The current population is roughly three times larger than the Domesday one . Such an increase is in fact quite small when it is borne in mind that England's population is estimated to have increased at least 20 times over the same period.

The slave population of 15 for an area the size of Pilton is reasonably typical of the West of England. For example at that time there was a total of 2100 in Somerset alone in 1086 They are thought to have been mainly estate workers working directly for the Abbot and his stewards. Although slaves could have been bought and sold it is likely that in practice their lifestyle was only slightly more arduous than other unfree peasants of the time. Indeed in some respects it may well have been better. As in years of shortage, the Abbot would have been in a much better position than the general population to provide food .

12

Domesday also tells us that there were 2 mills in Pilton; 46 acres of meadow; 40 acres of pasture, and a large area of woodland some one and a half miles long by three quarters of a mile wide. This relatively large amount of woodland was almost certainly scattered around the Parish rather than consisting of one large wood. The livestock is recorded as 4 cobs [riding horses], 35 cattle, 56 pigs, 42 she-goats and 500 sheep. The cattle would probably have been a mixture of beef cattle, cows and bulls for breeding but in addition there would have been 160 or so oxen for pulling the 20 ploughs. In Medieval times farmers knowledge and resources for over wintering cattle was severely limited [for example the growing of root vegetables for animals was not generally practised] and it was only the essential oxen and breeding animals which were kept for the following year. Any milk used was usually from ewes and goats rather than cows. The livestock figures given in Domesday would be a minimum as it is believed that they refer only to the Lord's livestock and excludes those of the villagers themselves. If these were included the figures would probably be twice as large.

There were 10 ploughs owned by The Lord and 10 by the villagers; as a rough approximation, a medieval plough was responsible for about 100 acres of arable land a year. If all ploughs were used in Pilton they would have been able to tend some 2000 acres. We can see from this that Pilton had a sizeable arable area, much more so than today. Approximately half of this arable land was farmed by the Abbot and half by the tenants of Pilton. The use of arable fields after harvest for grazing animals and the practice of half the fields remaining fallow each year provided some additional pasturage. The Domesday surveyors also state that there was additional potential arable land available, as much as could be used for 10 ploughs, or 1000 acres. Unfortunately it doesn't say what it was being used for at the time, but rough pasturage would be the most likely.

Domesday tells us that Pilton had two mills, neither of which have been identified with any certainty. One was probably in Ham in the far north of The Manor. The other was likely to have been just south of the Church. The succeeding mill still survives but has been reduced in height and is now used as out buildings to the house known as Monks Mill.

SECTION 3

==============MEDIEVAL==============

Medieval Society

From the Domesday Book onwards Pilton is blessed with a good number of documents which give interesting insights into its medieval life. We give some examples of the more important ones later in the next two sections.

Medieval society was somewhat alien to modern day ideas and ways of living. At its centre was the Manor, which was an area held by a Lord on sanction from The King. The medieval Manor of Pilton was re-formed shortly after 1066, and consisted of much the same area then as the present Pilton Civil Parish (see Section 2 for exceptions).Every Manor had its own Lord. For Pilton until 1539 the Lords were the various Abbots of Glastonbury. Overall control of their estates was through their stewards who in turn administered individual Manors through their bailiffs. It was the latter that most affected the people of Pilton on a day to day basis.

For most of the medieval era virtually all the people of Pilton were unfree peasants, there being only a handful of free-men. The tenants we shall be mentioning in the surveys came in this category.

A medieval plough with a half- team of 4 oxen,- the dress of the peasants , the plough, and the use of oxen for ploughing would have been a typical scene in the fields of Pilton in the 14th. century

14

Remnants of open field strips in 1809 can be seen to the east and west of Worthy Farm

The fact of them being unfree meant that there were various restrictions imposed upon them. They could not permanently leave the Manor without the Lord's permission, nor could they sue the Lord in the King's courts. If their daughters wished to marry, a fee had to be paid [known as merchet] as well as the Lord having to give his permission. On death, another fee was required (a heriot). In Pilton this was usually the best beast possessed by the deceased (invariably an ox), but if no beast was available it could be any valuable possession. All land was held `from the Lord', and a tenant had to attend the Manor Court and ask the Lords permission before he could pass his land on to his children.

> There were various labels for different classes in early Medieval society ,e.g. cottars, borders, villeins ,villagers, slaves

All the unfree tenants [and some free ones] had attached to their holding certain conditions or "work duties" as they were known. These involved compulsory work for the Lord and could be most arduous. In Pilton as in other agricultural areas the duties regularly covered the full range of farming activities e.g. mowing, harrowing, digging in the fields and vineyard, ploughing [often having to bring their own oxen], reaping, hoeing, repairing the Park's fence, carting produce to Glastonbury, accompanying monks on trips to Cornwall. The details of their duties were recorded in various surveys and we cover the two main ones for Pilton in section four.

The system of agriculture was particularly foreign to modern ways. All farmers were involved in arable farming as they tried to be self sufficient. An unusual feature of medieval farming however was that the arable producing areas were intermingled between all the tenants. Every holding was in the form of small strips of land each about an acre in size but four or five times longer than its width. A farmer might cultivate a dozen or more of these strips –depending on the size of his holding, but they would not all be together but spread around two very large fields. These fields were essentially open, that is there would be no hedges or other barriers between the strips. Even the arable strips of the Manorial Lord was intermingled with that of its tenants. The strips were grouped together to form blocks and the whole field might contain a dozen or more of these blocks, none of which would be fenced off from each other. This system of farming continued well past the medieval period because of the difficulties of unravelling the hundreds of strips into more

15

condensed and sensibly arranged holdings.

The map overleaf of a small area around Worthy Farm in 1809 shows the remnants of strip farming to the east and west of the farm. In Medieval times the strips would have been much longer, and part of Pilton's south field.

For central Pilton there were two of these large open fields, the North, and the South Fields. The precise location of them is unknown but approximately the South Field was south of an east-west line along Bread Street going southwards beyond Worthy Farm, and from the east boundary of the Deer Park eastwards towards the Fosse Way. The total area of the South Field was in the region of 3-400 acres, and the North Field had a similar acreage. Each year one field would be lying fallow, and after harvest the whole of the other was opened up for grazing. West and East Compton and Ham each had their own separate open fields.

The main arable crops were wheat and oats, for example in 1334 ; 156 acres of wheat was sown and 154 acres of oats, but only 5 acre of barley

The Manor Court was the main forum for organising the affairs of the Manor. All the Lord's unfree tenants had to attend and if they didn't they had to send their apologies. They took place in Pilton three or four times a year. The business of Pilton Court was usually presided over by the Glastonbury steward and a jury was elected from the local villagers. A varied range of transactions were dealt with. They recorded land transactions, and resolved disputes over property rights; they prosecuted recalcitrant tenants, and damage and trespass against the Lord's property; disputes between neighbours were also frequently dealt with. They discussed and levied fees due to the Lord when daughters married and tenants died. In Pilton as in other Glastonbury Manors, they were called "Hallemots" rather than" Court Barons" which was what they were known in much of the rest of England. The courts existed from the early days of Manorial organisation, but it was not until the 13th. Century that their proceedings were written down.

Only a few of the court proceedings relating to Pilton Manor have been translated.

Manor Courts

An extract of Pilton Manor Court Oct.14th. 1304

16

The Medieval ones which have been looked at start with a list of those villagers who have allowed their animals to stray. For example in 1262 Oggy Penni was fined 6d. for one of his calf's breaking into the Lord's meadow, and Peter of Bureford fined 6d. for his animals trespassing in the Lord's wood. In total at the 1262 court there were 16 different villagers whose animals had offended and consequently fined 3d. or 6d. a time. The total number of offenders could however be considerably more

Sowing the fields
c. 14th. Century.

than this, and in 1304 there was a mass break out of animals with 55 different villagers being fined. The main `offenders' would seem to have been the oxen with as many as 108 being mentioned as part of the breakout. Of these there were eleven separate villagers each being fined for six oxen. This number, six, is interesting as the standard plough team number is generally considered to be eight oxen. Possibly a smaller number was sufficient for ploughing in Pilton, or it may have been a means of avoiding work duties.

At a court in 1283 one of the offenders was a *Robert at Worthy* (fined 3d. for 6 beasts in the cornfield), confirming that Worthy was a named place of residence as early as the 13th. Century. Similarly this also applies to Burford.

Osbert of Bureford was chairman of the Jury at the 1262 court and he announces that two proceeds of Heriot [a form of death duty] were due to the Lord, one was the usual best beast which in this case was an ox, but the other was due from Richard at Holt who didn't

have a best beast and so paid in corn. There was also discussion about one villager who tried to conceal his duty to give Heriot but it was unclear whether or not he was additionally fined because of the concealment.

Near to the end of the 1262 court proceedings came the important matter of land transactions. Seven of the existing tenants gave money and promised rents for various separate pieces of land .Taking two examples, Robert of Hamme paid 9s. and agreed to 3s. annual rent for a piece of meadow near Herty, and Joannes of Westlegh acquired 15 acres of arable [place not specified but presumably in the common fields]. All the seven transactions involved land which was already in the possession of the Lord. This was unusual and it is possible that at that time The Lord was trying to reduce the amount of land he directly farmed. The more usual land transaction involved a tenant first giving up his land ' into the hands of The Lord ' and then, after payment of a fee, it would be immediately regranted to a new tenant, the new tenant usually being a son or other close relation of the retiring tenant. For example at the 1265 Court, Enid, widow of Osbert Oggi surrendered her holding namely half a virgate [20 acres]of arable land for which Walter her son thence gave 50s. This was the principal way of transferring land between generations for many centuries. At first the proceedings were recorded only as part of the normal record keeping of the court and solely for the Lord's own purposes. Gradually however as the

King's Courts came to compete with the Manor courts an additional copy was made and given to the tenants as proof of title. He or she became a copyholder.

> A fine of 3d. represented an average of one or two days wages for an agricultural labourer in the 14th Century.

Tenants could also be fined if it was thought that they were shirking their work dues, and at a 1304 court Robert Albus was fined 3d. because he badly mowed the meadow.

The court was also the place where the traditional work duties were agreed, and, no doubt disputed. For example at the same 1304 court all those tenants with a ferdella of land [10 acres] swore on oath that such a holding had required from ancient times, that they must help reap 5 acres of corn every Autumn. Eleven of the customary tenants had been trying to get out of this duty and were fined amounts as much as 3s.

One of the medieval impositions on unfree villagers was the need to obtain the Lord's permission and pay him a fee if a daughter was to marry. There are three such requests at the Easter court of 1265, Christine, daughter of Edward Hywan pays 2s. for the permission, Robert Upehamme pays 8s. for his daughter Celia, and our old friend Oggy Penny pays half a mark [6s. 8d.]for his daughter Edith. It is not clear why the above amounts should vary so much, though one of the factors was if the bride was marrying outside of the Manor. If the Lord was to lose the potential for future workers he would expect to be compensated .

At every Easter court there was an enumeration of all the adult males of Pilton who were not in possession of their own land. There were 92 of them listed in 1265, and they had to pay 6d each, but a few were let off as they were too poor. It would seem that this was a form of Poll Tax on the non-land holding labour, and enabled the Lord to profit from those who were not otherwise paying anything to him.

Tithings

An important part of medieval life was the system of tithings. Every male from the age of twelve had to belong to one, and each tithing was held responsible for the lawful actions of each of its members. Thus if one of its members stole from any other member of the Manor it was the whole tithing's duty to assist in bringing him to justice, and if necessary compensate the victim. The tithing was in effect a self policing group. The head was known as the tithingman who was expected to present at the hundred court all major public nuisances and criminal misdeeds in his area eg. robbery, murder, assault, poaching, breaches of the peace, trading offences and obstructing the King's highway.

If a person witnessed a crime he or she was duty bound to raise the hue and cry (e.g. by shouting out Stop! Thief!) and all within earshot had to join in and assist in bringing the perpetrator to justice. There were penalties for not raising the hue and cry and also for raising it wrongly.

The Hundred Court took place in open ground on a hill east of Cannards Grave. The Hundred took its name *Whitestone* from a large white stone on this hill. In bad weather it retired to Shepton Mallet and later the court was established permantly at the Swan Inn in Kilver Street. Also included in the Hundred were the parishes of Batcombe, Croscombe, Ditcheat, Doulting, Downhead, Hornblotton, Lamyatt, East Pennard, Pylle, Shepton Mallet and Stoke-Lane.

Although the system of tithings and hundreds date back to Saxon times, the first documentary mention of the Whitestone Hundred is in the Domesday book. At that time the whole of Pilton was in this Hundred, however, in the following centuries various Abbots expanded their own special Hundred (The Glastonbury XII Hides) into the western parts of Pilton. In 1505 the boundary between the two hundreds went through the middle of Pilton park up to the south door of the church, out through the north door, and then northwards for half a mile before veering westwards to North Wootton.(see appendix for more detail).

The original tithing comprised ten households but as populations increased this number was invariably exceeded. For Pilton the whole manor was divided into only four tithings 1)Westholme and Holte, 2) Pilton, 3) East and West Compton, 4) Ham, the first being in the Glastonbury XII hides and the other three in the Whitestone Hundred,

The boundary or mere stone between the two Hundreds is still outside the Church doors on the old path going to the Manor House

SECTION 4

=======MEDIEVAL SURVEYS ,ACCOUNTS====

Survey of Henry de Sully 1189

Henry de Sully became Abbot of Glastonbury in 1189 and immediately commissioned a survey of the Abbey's lands to assist him in managing his estate. This was a survey of most, if not all the Abbey's estates but only some of the results have survived. Pilton's is amongst the survivors but there is one page of the original manuscript which has been lost. Nevertheless the survey gives an interesting insight into Pilton's early medieval work practices.

[e.g. Walter at the Ford, William of theMoor, Hugo of Compton, Sewinas of Pilton, Joseph of Ham]; or their occupation [e.g. Osbertus the merchant, Henry the Smith, Ernis the Reeve, William the Carpenter]. At other times the

Harrowing the fields after sowing

The survey was conducted at a time when the use of surnames had yet to become generally accepted practice, and before they were hereditary. Most tenants therefore are referred to by their Christian name only e.g. Vincent, Radulphus, Hugo, Garmund. Where a second name is used it often refers to the area where they came from

added identifier is the father's name, e.g. Robert son of Henry, Robert son of Richard, Robert son of Herding. In many of these examples we can see the basis of how surnames developed.

20

It is also worth noting that both East Compton and West Compton are directly referred to in the survey as sub areas of Pilton, showing that they were well established by at least the 12th. Century. However there is no mention at this time of the area of Westholme or of East Town.

The survey's main purpose was to record all the work duties of the tenants, the amount of land they held, and all payments that were due from the holding. An example of one of the survey's entries is as follows:

At West Compton Adam son of Oggis, young Oggis,Hubertus son of Oggis, Herdwine,

A typical Medieval cart

Osbert son of Ailward, Oggis senior, Alward Rider, Osbert son of Aluric, Sewi the Merchant, each hold half a virgate[20 acres]for forty pence and a gift. They each plough half an acre one day a week from Michaelmas [29th. Sept.] to Christmas. One perch one day a week from Epiphany [Jan 6th.]to the Annunciation of the Blessed Virgin Mary [march 25th.].Each week from Hockday to the feast of St. John [approx. 8 months] half an acre. They hoe when the work needs doing, reap three times, sow three times, carry, cart hay, and harvests when the work needs doing, they thresh, dig in the vineyard, they do suit at the mill.

These work services are reasonably typical of what all the tenants had to perform throughout the year with variations according to the size of holding .Also each piece of land had slightly different traditions associated with it. The mention of *'a gift'* is the Monk's euphemism for a compulsory donation which was levied on the whole Manor and then divided between certain tenants according to their land holding. In total the whole manor `gifted' 73 shillings four pence, quite a tidy

sum for those times

The vineyard mentioned was almost certainly in Pilton and gives us an early date for its existence. That digging is specified as needed in the vineyard suggests possibly that the vineyard was still in the process of being set up.

To `*do suit at the mill'* means that when grain needed milling a tenant could only use the Lord's Mill, not anyone else's or even his own hand mill at home.

Naturally there was a fee he had to pay for doing this.

The mixture of money payments and work duties were reasonably typical of the times, but as the medieval period progressed work dues declined and money payments increased.

The survey itself lists 69 different tenants occupying some 1175 acres of ground. Because of the missing sheet it is not possible to give any exact figures for the whole Manor.

Summary of Holdings

1 tenant with	60a.	
12 tenants "	40 a.	
11 " "	20 a.	
41 " "	10 a.	
1 " "	5 a	
3 "	unspecified	

It is seen that the most common holding amounted to 10 acres, and this would have been arable land in the open fields. Because of the two field system being operated, only 5 acres each year would have been available for growing crops, and given the poor yields of the time there was precious little excess to sell at market in order to pay the rent. However there was available to each tenant additional common pasture for sheep and cattle, as well as common meadows.

Of the listed 69 tenants four of them were widows and they had exactly the same work duties to perform as men. In practice however both male and female tenants could get their children to perform the work, or if they could afford it, pay someone to do it. Indeed it was usual for sons to stay at home until they could find their own land. They either helped on the family farm or hired themselves out as farm labourers.

Only seven free men are mentioned in the survey, otherwise all the tenants were tied to Pilton and unable to leave without the Lords permission.

> One historian estimated the missing page contained details about 5 tenants holding 10 acres, and 8 holding 20 acres. If so this would gve us an overall total of 82 tenants holding about 1400 acres of arable land.

Survey of Abbot Ford c. 1260

Roger Ford was Abbot between 1252 and 1261 and although the exact date of finalising his survey is unknown it was probably towards the later part of his reign.. The survey is along similar lines to the one made 71 years previously, and is mainly concerned with the detailed work duties and payments of Pilton's tenants. A typical entry is:

Osbertus of Bureford holds half a virgate [20 acres] of land for 36d per annum, gives 12d. to the larder,Peterspenny 1d., to the vineyard 2d., and ploughs and threshes, leads the sowing and harrowing of 5 acres of winter crop which is worth 21 1/2 d., and threshes seed at the same place - worth 1 1/2 d. He ploughs 2 acres 3 perch for oats - worth 9d.. He fallows 5 acres - worth 15d., and comes to 4 workdays with 8 oxen if he has them, worth 16d.. He comes to the same place for 4 days with 1 carthorse or ox - worth 2 1/4d.He comes with his horse to harrowing when required. Collects brushwood at Baltonsborough - worth 1d.,and weeds for 2 days - worth ½ d. ,and in the Park fences 32 feet - worth 4d. every 20 years. He mows in the meadow for 5 days and has nothing - worth 5d.,and carries hay with a cart for 4 days-worth 6d., makes hayricks for 1 day-worth 1/2d. He reaps 3 acres for 3 days and shall have nothing-worth 9d., comes with a half cart to carry the Lords hay and corn.....worth 7 1/2d........he works equally at Pilton and Glastonbury. He carries millstones to the Mill with 19 fellows-worth 1/4d. and carries hay from Hunimede [in Wootton] to Glastonbury.

A peasant threshes the sheave with a jointed flail

When he had finished the Lord's work he was free to tend his own land! Osbertus served as a model, and the other 20 acre holders had similar duties.

A few explanations may help to clarify some of the items. The payment ' to the Larder' is for supplies to the Abbey at Glastonbury and is the same item as the unspecified gift mentioned in the previous survey. Peter's penny was originally a tribute to St. Peters in Rome but whether the Abbot passed it on or kept it for the Abbey's own use isn't known. The phrase attached to some work duties "...he has nothing....." refers to the fact that some tenants were traditionally provided with food if they performed certain activities., but here the Lord is making clear that this tradition is not operating.

One of the most interesting features of this survey compared to the 1189 one is that the majority of the work duties of the tenants have been valued and for the appropriate payment they could opt out of the works. We are seeing here the beginnings of the erosion of standard feudal work practices and further steps to a more modern money economy.

The duty to work in the vineyard has been replaced by a payment of 2d., which either means that the work itself was no longer required or the work was more effectively done by other labour sources such as women or youths .

Summary of Holdings

1 tenant	with	40 a.
3 tenants	"	30 a.
33	"	"	20 a.
31	"	"	10 a.
4	"	"	5 a.
1	"	"	2 a.
2	"	house only

The total number of land holders was 73 plus 2 householders. They accounted for approximately 1122 acres of arable land.

In this survey the lands farmed for the sole use of the Lord [The Demesne] are listed.

There were 863 acres mostly arable but some of which was pasture .There was an additional 75 acres of meadow and more than 135 acres of mixed woodland and pasture. The Lords arable was intermingled with the holdings of his tenants. These areas are similar to those mentioned in a later survey of 1315 which lists 687 acres of arable, 1071/2 acres of meadow, plus extensive pasture land, woodlands and moor.

The field names are also given and divided between the two open fields the South and North. Amongst the more interesting ones are *la Worth'* which was part of *the south field* and the Lord had 31 acres there. Also in the south field was *la Holte* where he had 120 acres plus a wood of 52 acres. It is also indicated that at that time there existed an old stone barn which if so would have been before the surviving Abbey barn which was not built until later in the 14th. Century

Other names mentioned in the survey which survive to this day are Bureford and Stodleigh (Stoodly Lane)

It is from this survey that we learn of William Aurifaber (Goldsmith) who had wide ranging duties for the Monks . He had to supply a boat for 8 men and ferry the Abbot, plus various provisions, hunters and dogs and wine, between Glastonbury and La Bowe (the bridge on the A 361 west of Steanbow) He also had to police the waterways against the fishing for eels and whiting in Hercy Moor. Clearly the waterway between Pilton and Glastonbury was navigatable at that time.

Reeve's Accounts

The position of Reeve was a Manorial office served by a peasant who had been elected to the position by his fellow peasants.

Part of the first line of the 1330 Reeve's account

The office was an arduous one as he was responsible for ensuring not only that all work duties were performed but for the agricultural activities of the Lord's Farm, what crops were to be sown, on what days, and when harvested. In addition he collected the Lord's rents, bought and sold the Farm's output, and had to account for every penny he spent throughout the year. These accounts were audited yearly and written up by the Abbot's scribe, the Reeve himself seldom being able to write. The year ran from September to September and a partial translation has been made for the year 1330/31. Despite only a part being available it is nevertheless full of interest.

In the year 1330/1 he collected over £37 in rents . The individual rents varied from a few pennies to a few pounds so it is not possible to say how many people this involved, but from other sources it was probably in the region of 150 different tenants . They were often collected from each tenant two or three times a year and so this rent collection duty alone was not a light one. We also learn that he himself was excused some rent payments because of his duties and this also applied to a few of his helpers such as the shepherds, some ploughmen and drovers and the swine herd keeper.

We saw in the previous survey that tenants were allowed to get out of their work services by making a payment in lieu. Twenty did so that year [usually about 8 shillings per tenant] thus adding to the amount of rent received. We also learn that the year was a bad one for nuts and acorns so the Reeve was unable to collect any money from this source.

There were clearly large building works going on at both Pilton and Glastonbury [involving new or the extending of chapels], and because of this many of the Lord's oxen were tied up carting stone as well as there being less labour available to the Reeve for agricultural purposes. The works must have been extensive as oxen from *Dycheat* and *Melles* were also being used in the carting.

One gets the feeling that the Reeve was pleased with himself when he managed to get as much as 12 shillings for one worn out ox and 13s 4d. for two weakened cows. He also bemoans the fact that he was unable to sell the nettles from the Manor House garden as they were used by the Lord's oxen. Nothing was wasted. He accounted for £5-8s. obtained from Manor Court fines and a further £6-13s. from tenants' payments for being granted their land holding. He sold cheese to the Reeves of *Melles Markesbury, Pennard, Batecombe,Doulting* and *Baltonesburgh*. Virtually all of his buying and selling with other Glastonbury Manors was by tally.

He was also responsible for accounting for the various gifts made to the

Tally sticks were a common method of settling Medieval transactions.Long squared hazel sticks had notches cut into them according to an agreed coding system recording the amount.The stick was then split into two.Each party kept half and before settlement of the account the two halves would be matched

poor at Christmas and other festivals ,thus that year he provided 8 gallons of cider for the Christmas. Festivities. He also was responsible for repairing the ploughs and carts and buying new ones when necessary. In the year he spent 12d. for a new plough share and purchased 7lb. of grease for one of the wagons carrying stone for the building works. This was exceptional however, as seven wagons in more normal use accounted for only 17 lbs. of grease.

He sold 106 pigeons by two tallies valued at 2s. 11d to the Reeve at Dycheaghete, and overall he made 20s. profit for the year on dovecote sales.

A surprisingly low number of horses were part of the farm, only 3 mares are mentioned plus 3 foals of 3 years of age and two foals of which one was a female of 2 years and another a female still being milked. This attention to the details of husbandry is typical to the whole of the accounts. Thus for other animals such as cows and sheep and pigs the ages and where necessary the sex are listed.

The Reeve accounted for 48 oxen and in the year he sent 8 off to the Larder at Glastonbury and sold one, leaving the estate 39 to keep over the winter. Interestingly only 2 cows existed plus one calf and one of these was soon sold. The most numerous animals were sheep of which there were 387 of various categories; 152 ewes, 86 lambs, 98 hogs 45 wethers and 6 rams. Only 11 were diseased ,

much better than in 1274 when 83 were found to be diseased .He started the year with 56 pigs, but a few were diseased , two were used up for the advent of the new Abbot and another 16 were sent on to Glastonbury.

Glastonbury Chartulary

A further source of information on medieval Pilton is the Glastonbury Chartulary published by The Somerset Record Society. It covered all the Glastonbury estates and amongst its contents are several deeds relating to properties in Pilton. One of them involves a Peter of Yadewyk in 1270 giving back to Glastonbury 10 1/2 acres of land in East Compton. The land is split equally between the two open fields of East Compton namely the East Field and the West Field.

Various of the deeds spell out agreements between tenants and Glastonbury where the tenants swap their common rights in some lands for exclusive use of other lands thus enabling them to enclose the land. Although the acreages involved were not very large , the deeds illustrate that from as early as 13th century rationalisation of the open field agricultural system was underway. For example in 1243 William Topinael and his wife give up all their common rights in Pilton Park and Eastholt in exchange for 15 acres of meadow and woodland.

Some small rationalisation of the Feudal services are also illustrated in The Chartulary. For example in 1264 Abbot Robert of Petherton remitted all services which Richard Westleya and his ancestors were accustomed to undertake. The services included carting wheat and hay to Pilton Court, hay from Honymed' meadow to Glastonbury, transporting monks to Cornwall, supervising Autumn ploughing. In exchange Richard gives up 10 acre of land and agrees to pay an increased rent of 10d. per annum.

SECTION 5

===============PILTON PARK===============

The Medieval era was one of extreme ostentation, at least for those who could afford it. Any Lord who wanted the respect of his peers had to exhibit his worth, and one of the ways of doing this was to make a deer park. Glastonbury Abbey had four [of which Pilton's was the first], and should you think this a little excessive the Bishops of Wells had as many as eight at various times, one of which was next door at Evercreech.

The precise year of setting up Pilton Park is not known. It probably didn't exist in 1189 but it certainly did by 1227. In that year there was a legal case about it when a widow took the Abbot of Glastonbury to court as she felt that the emparkment deprived her of her grazing rights. Our best estimate is that it was laid out sometime between the years 1220 and 1227.

The Park was located in the south west corner of the Manor, south of the main Pilton to Glastonbury road.(see Map). Although most of the boundary is known with some confidence there is some uncertainty about whether the park fence also enclosed the Manor House.

The total length of the perimeter was some 4.7 miles in circuit and enclosed 580 acres, making it more than twice as large as most deer parks of the time.

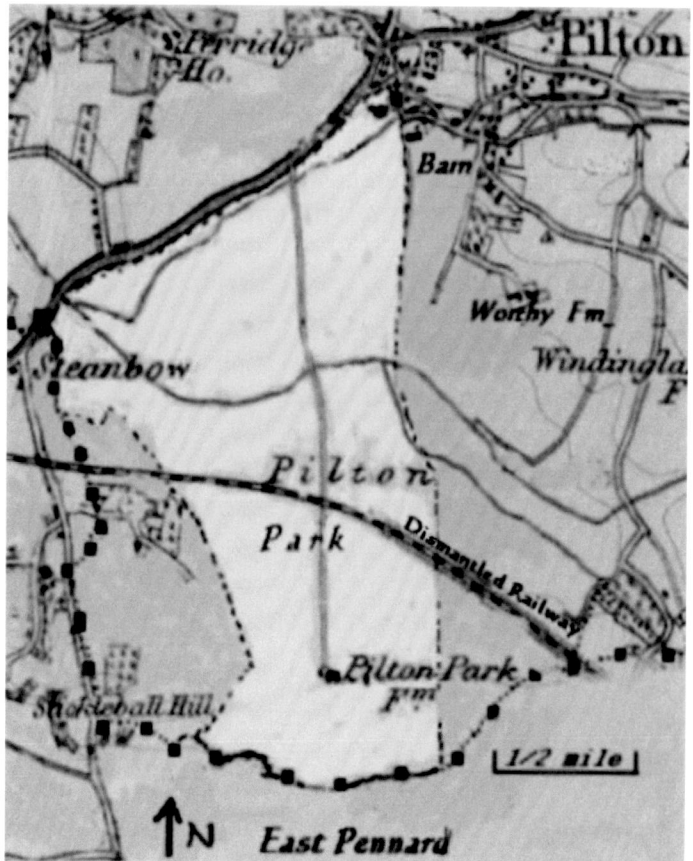

Pilton Park marked on a 1940's O.S. map

26

The usual shape for deer parks were round or oval as these minimised the expensive perimeter fence while maximising the area available for the deer to graze in. Clearly the Monks had not read the text book as Pilton's shape was a somewhat irregular rectangle. One of the irregularities of the boundary is due to a later addition. Sometime between 1323 and 1334 Abbot Adam of Sodbury " ...... detached a large parcel of wood called Le Nyeholt from the common and added it to Pilton Park....." This was in the north west corner of the park.

A survey made in 1536 recorded 351 deer but the type of deer is not specified. Most probably they were fallow deer as they are reckoned to be the easiest to manage in captivity and their venison the tastiest.

certainly have been where Pilton Park Farm House used to stand. Indeed there was a farm there called Lodge Farm in the 18th. Century.

The means of building and maintaining the perimeter fence was interesting as it involved using labour from twenty different Manors [see appendix for full details],some of whom came from over 20 miles away. They didn't even get paid for the work as it was included in their work duties, and if they didn't do it they had to pay the Monks for this privilege. The fence was placed on top of a continuous 6 feet earth and stone mound, and some remains of this mound can still be seen today on the south and west sides of the Park.

Before it was demolished, a view of Pilton Park Farm from the top of Pennard Hill looking north.

The ground used for the Park was probably semi waste and previously used for common grazing. The area was much more extensively wooded than today. Any emparked area however must contain water for the deer and this was well provided by two good size streams.

Within the park there was likely to have been a hunting lodge. If so it would almost

Hunting the deer took place by two means. Either they were driven by beaters past a hiding place and slain on foot by bow and arrow, or hunted on horses with the aid of hounds. We know the monks kept hounds for this purpose as Abbot Ford's survey records them being transported to and from Glastonbury by water to Steanbow, the Whitelake being navigable at the time.

At the dissolution of the monasteries in 1539 the park and manor passed to the crown. It was described by Henry VIII's assessors at the time as having its palings in good condition. In 1540 Edward Rogers was installed as keeper of the park for a payment of 2d.a day, with `.....herbage and pannage in the same park.....and of Parkhill.....and other parcels of land lying within the same park....' The letter of installation suggests that much of the Park was probably given over to agricultural use by this time. A survey in 1552 suggests that the Park may already have been diminished with its circumference reduced to 2 miles.

In 1547 the park was acquired by Edward Seymour, Duke of Somerset, then lost by him in 1549, regained in 1550,and lost finally together with his head in 1552.Then it passed to Seymour's son ,also Edward, but as he was a minor his property was administered by the Court of Wards. They didn't look after it too well and a letter in 1555 described the park and palings as being in `......great decay....'

However in 1555 it still had some of its deer, and for a number of years they attracted gangs of poachers. Numerous poaching expeditions were made in the years 1553-5 which resulted eventually in a number of battles with the park keeper and his men. On one occasion the poachers went equipped to poach with four greyhounds, longbows, crossbows, a pike, a Welsh Hook and long wooden staves. The keeper and his men were ready and pursued them, with arrows fired by both sides. The only stated casualty was the killing of one of the poachers [John Alanne] by bow and arrow. Clearly poaching was a serious business in those times.

Although probably much smaller than when it was first set up , the park remained in existence until the latter half of the 17th. Century. The land was then given over entirely to agricultural use and combined with other land farmed by the Lord to form the Pilton Park Estate.(see section 8 for its later history)

Part of a 1607 map of Somerset showing Pilton Park between Norwood Park (also Glatonbury's) to the west, and the Bishops Park at Evercreech to the east

SECTION 6

=============MANORIAL LORDS===========

The Seymours

In 1539 the main monasteries were closed down. On November 19th.of that year Abbot Whiting was executed on Glastonbury Torr and The Crown took possession of Pilton Manor. 800 years or so of monastic ownership was ended. Interestingly it was Thomas Whiting the brother of the Abbot who at the time was the tenant of the Lord's Home Farm at Pilton including The Manor House and Park.

By 1539 the medieval traditions concerning unfree people had nearly died out throughout most of England. In the monastic Manors however they lingered on longer than average, and when the Crown took over Pilton Manor there were still 22 bondmen left in Pilton.There was still at least one left in 1564 when Sir Edward Seymour granted a bondman his freedom.

We covered in the last section the history of the Park, part of which is also that of the Manor. From 1539 until 1547 the Manor remained in the Crowns Hands. When it was

At the Dissolution, the Glastonbury Abbey steward, Sir Thomas Speke had overall control of Pilton and he retained this position afterwards.

granted to Edward Seymour. He owned Pilton on and off, until his execution in 1552. Pilton along with his other lands went back to the State, but as his son [also Edward] was a minor, it was the Ward of Courts which administered the estate. The position was however complicated by the fact that Edward's mother the Duchess of Somerset was also one of the wards, and in addition retained widow's rights over some of her husband's properties. One of these properties is thought to have been Pilton. The Seymours' interest in Pilton may therefore have been continuous throughout the 1550's.

In any case by January 1559 Queen Elizabeth had restored all of Edward's lands. Pilton was firmly back in his hands, and he became Lord of The Manor. He retained this position until his death in 1621. This Edward outlived his two sons and the next Lord of Pilton was his grandson William, the Royalist Commander in the Civil War.(died 1660)

29

According to some authorities William's penalty for ending on the losing side was the forfeit of his lands. However William was certainly Pilton's Lord in 1647, and the Lordship was still in his grandson's hands in 1662 & 1670.

Again the father outlived the eldest son Henry, who would normally have inherited the Lordship. So it then passed first to Henry's son William who died in 1671, unmarried, then back to grandfather William's younger son John who died childless in 1675. There being no more male heirs the Lordship of Pilton then passed to the female side of the family, Elizabeth, daughter of the above mentioned Henry. She married Thomas Bruce in 1676. Thus, after over 120 years with a named Seymour in control of Pilton, its Lordship changed hands.

The Bruce's

Elizabeth Seymour, as granddaughter of William the 2nd. Duke of Somerset, inherited many estates and Pilton was not her principal one. There is no evidence even of her and Thomas residing at Pilton on a permanent basis. Elizabeth's marriage to Thomas Bruce seemed to result in a joint Lordship until she died in 1696.

Thomas Bruce [also 2nd. Earl of Ailesbury] then became sole Lord. However he was often in trouble over his gambling debts and started to sell off parts of the Manor to raise money. In 1690 he sold to his sister Lady Isabella Bruce the Park and main farm together with the Manor house for £2,000. The properties were only on a 99 year lease. Shortly afterwards Lady Isabella traded in the property for an annuity and the estate passed to Edward Rider.

From around 1700 onwards Thomas started to sell lands in earnest. Before 1690 he possessed not only The Park and its associated farms but over 100 other different properties and farms in Pilton itself. When he came to sell The Manor in 1719 there were less than 30.

Traditionally one of the means by which a Lord exerted influence over his subjects had been his control over land ownership. After 1719 therefore Pilton's Lords influence was much diminished.

The Langtons & Gores

Joseph Langton bought the Manor and its associated properties for £2615 in 1719, although this sale price also included a few properties in North Wootton. His property holdings in Pilton itself were relatively modest but his main estate was elsewhere, and he did not reside in Pilton

The Manor remained in his family until 1783. It then changed hands by the marriage of Bridget Langton, the daughter and sole heiress of Joseph Langton to William Gore. Upon obtaining such wealth it was only right that William should change his name to Gore-Langton and the Lordship of Pilton remained with his heirs until the 1890's. The Gore-Langtons continued the practice of the previous Lords of Pilton and resided outside of the Manor.

Rights of Lordship are now so diminished as to be of little account; however some people still value the title. As recently as June 1996 the Lordship of the Manor of Pilton was sold by auction for £7,500 to a buyer wishing to remain anonymous.

30

SECTION 7

===========WAR & REBELLION===========

Civil War

Long term differences of opinion between Charles I and Parliament eventually led in 1642 to open conflict between the two sides. The King's attempts to impose taxation without the consent of parliament together with changes in forms of religious worship led to widespread opposition throughout England. Religious discontent was particularly strong in Somerset as many of the cloth workers were Puritans who objected strongly to the King's 'reforms'. From early on in the conflict the two sides were given nicknames, the Royalists being popularly known as Cavaliers (from the Spanish word Caballeros meaning armed trooper or horseman), and the Parliamentarians known as Roundheads (a reference to the shaved heads of the London Apprentices who actively supported Parliament.

With the exception of Wells, most of the population of the local area favoured Parliament, the Royalists being viewed as outsiders. However the majority in all areas tried to keep out of the conflict and gave very little active support for either side.

William Seymour Lieutenant General in the west of the Kings forces

31

In July 1642 King Charles sent William Seymour, the Marquis of Hertford into Somerset to rally support for the Royalist cause. He was appointed as overall commander of the King's forces at the beginning of the war. Pilton had a special interest in the Marquis as he was at the time Lord of Pilton Manor. Few ever credited William Seymour with being a great soldier, and he was appointed more for his social and financial status plus his local influence rather than his military experience. Before the end of 1644 he had been honourably `retired' to a place on the King's Council at Oxford.

When he reached Somerset he based himself at Wells which was strongly supportive of The King. On August 1st. a street brawl broke out at Shepton Mallet when Hertford's second- in- command, Sir Ralph Hopton with a small force confronted Colonel William Strode, who had called out the local militia for Parliament. Initially The Cavaliers gained control of the situation and Colonel Strode was arrested and handed over to the local Constable. However when news was received of large masses of local population on their way to relieve Strode, Sir Hopton withdrew back to Wells, Colonel Strode being immediately released.

Shortly afterwards another attempt was made by the Royalists to visit Shepton but with a larger force. They were met halfway between Wells and Shepton (on the old Wells road outside of Croscombe) by Colonel Strode and his men. Another fracas developed and this time a dozen or so men were injured or killed, before Hopton retired back to Wells.

More importantly another skirmish of the conflict took place on 4 August 1642 at Marshall's Elm just outside Street. On this occasion the Royalist forces predominated against inexperienced Parliamentarians who suffered 27 dead and 60 being taken prisoner.

Despite this success the Cavaliers' situation was precarious, being generally outnumbered in the area. They consequently withdrew to safer places.

The Civil war had come early to Somerset as it wasn't until the 22nd. August that Charles raised his standard at Nottingham and openly called upon his supporters to fight against Parliament's forces. The first major battle nationally took place outside of the West of England at Edgehill on the 23rd. October of the same year.

Apart from the skirmishes already mentioned there was no large scale fighting either in Pilton itself or in the immediate area, The nearest major battle being at Langport. However both sides occupied and controlled the area around Pilton at various times during the War. It was the demands for provisions and billeting from both armies which were a major drain on local resources.

For example, Colonel Jepson, a Parliamentarian leader, quartered his regiment in Somerset for 4 months between December 1645 and March 1646. Pilton residents were forced to provide quarters for 40 of his men at regular times during this period, none paying in cash and leaving maybe only a signed ticket for their stay. Also there was regular plundering of horses , carts and livestock by both sides throughout the period. Parliament eventually settled, but not until three years later. Even after fighting had ceased, across

Seymour was only fined rather than executed for his support of the King. Initially the fine was fixed at £12,603, the value of two years' income from all his estates. On appeal in 1648 it was reduced to £8,345 but there is no record that the fine was ever paid.

Somerset there were widespread disturbances between locals and soldiers, as the latter continued to have free lodgings. This led to a number of riots throughout the County. In Pilton itself repeated rioting took place, and a number of killings occurred.

April 1646 saw the last of the fighting in the West, and Charles was executed in 1649.

The Monmouth Rebellion

When Charles II died in February 1685, his legal heir James became King. However he was a Catholic and many influential people preferred Charles's illegitimate son The Duke of Monmouth, who was Protestant. In 1680 he made a highly successful tour around the West Country, and many thousands turned out to cheer him. This encouraged him to believe he had a strong base upon which to launch an attempt on the Crown. He returned to Lyme Regis on the 11th. June 1685 and marched into Somerset, picking up an assorted group of agricultural workers. He pronounced himself King of England at Taunton on June 18th.

> Monmouth had few experienced soldiers and most of his fighters consisted of men armed only with clubs, pitchforks and suchlike. Hence the Rebellion's popular name –The Pitchfork Rebellion.

Around 23rd. June, with a force of some 4,000 or so men he marched through Pilton to Shepton Mallet, then on towards Bath. However he turned back from Bath after hearing of the imminent arrival of large numbers of King James forces coming to meet him.

He returned to Shepton, and then via Wells continued to Sedgemoor. The King's forces took the route to Sedgemoor going through Pilton, giving Piltonians the opportunity of seeing both armies during the space of a few weeks .

The showdown came on 6th. July at Weston Zoyland in Sedgemoor. No match for the King's trained troops, Monmouth's scratch forces were routed. 500 were killed and 1500 taken prisoner. Many thousands of the rebels had fled the battlefield before the cessation of hostilities.

By then Monmouth himself had fled. He was found two days later disguised as a shepherd, taken prisoner and transported to London. There was no need for a trial as Monmouth had already been condemned as a traitor by Act of Parliament. He was brought to Tower Hill and beheaded on the 15th. July.

The tracking down of Monmouth's supporters began. One of the means was by using village constables to list all people away from their homes during the rebellion. As many as 4,000 names were collected from the various West Country areas, but only one, a certain George Duncarton came from Pilton . He was never found and it is presumed he was a casualty at Sedgemoor. This active support for Monmouth was low compared to some surrounding villages. Croscombe for example had 14 rebels listed, and there were 5 in West Pennard.

The aftermath was nearly as bloody as the battle itself, and certainly more famous. The subsequent trials known as the `Bloody Assizes' were ruled over by the notorious Judge Jefferies. 320 of those who supported Monmouth were condemned to death and a further 800 transported to the West Indies to serve as slaves for up to ten years.

SECTION 8

==============TWO MANSIONS==============

The Manor House

The two most important buildings in most Manors were invariably the Church and where the Lord lived i.e. the Manor House. We have already noted (section 6) that it would seem that none of the post dissolution Lords lived in the Manor on a permanent basis, and before that the Abbots of Glastonbury's main residence was naturally the Abbey itself. Because of this the importance of the Manor House in Pilton's history is perhaps diminished compared to some other large Manors.

Originally built in the time of Michael of Amesbury, 1235-52, it was refurbished by Abbot Adam of Sodbury 1323-34, added to by Abbot John Chinock 1375-1420 and later by Edward Earl of Hertford. Edward Andrews a Bristol merchant largely rebuilt it c. 1754 and there are later 19th. century additions

It was described in 1315 as being set in 17 acres of garden and orchard. and in 1539 it was described as having a 'feyr *curtilage walled with a feyr gatehouse, a feyr open hall with hearth, 2 porches, 10 feyr chambers, a long chappell with bellhops, a wyne cellar, a pretty pantry and butry, a feyr kitchen and larder, a bakehouse, a washhouse, a stabull for 10 horses, a fair pichyn*

Line Drawing of the Manor House

34

house and orchard and garden adjoining the parke .....'

The Manor House is close to the Church and to the south-west.. An 1809 plan of the area shows two buildings to the south of the entrance (see the plan in section 10). The first would have been the gatehouse or lodge and the second, on the banks of the stream, possibly the chapel, both now demolished. Due probably to the house always being let to tenants rather than being the residence of the Lord of the Manor, it was not always maintained in good repair. Henry Hope bought it in 1808 and his surveyor was not particularly impressed by it:.`......the house is on a small scale and does not appear to ever have been a mansion of consequence.......the inside of the Mansion is in a very bad state and can not be made habitable for less than £1000......' (see appendix for more detail).

At one time there were two dovecotes attached to the property. One was up the hill on the other side of the stream [probably close to the Abbey Barn] and was in existence as long ago as 1260 but now long disappeared. The other is still in existence and is to the west of the main house. Its building timbers have been dated to around 1440, and when originally built it contained 811 nesting holes. The picture shows the interior of the dovecote with its nesting holes in the west wall. At the time of the picture the dovecote was used as a general storeroom.

The Manor House and Manorial Lordship were both in Lord Bruce's hands until 1690 when the House and accompanying estate was sold on a 99 year lease to Lord Bruce's sister. From this time onwards the affairs of Lordship and the Manor House were separate, although Lord Bruce still remained the freeholder.

Lord Bruce's sister traded in the estate nine years later to Edward Rider for an annuity of £200 per annum .The Manor House and its associated lands were heavily mortgaged and Edward Rider and his heirs had to do much juggling of finances in order to keep possession of the estate. In 1705 Lord Bruce sold the freehold of the estate to John Smith .

Despite his financial difficulties the estate was still in Rider's hands when it was sold in 1754 to Edward Andrews, a Bristol merchant. He passed it to his son Colonel Edward Andrews who was mainly responsible for the building we see today. He sold it to Henry Hope in September 1808 who settled it on his niece Henrietta Maria Sarah Pole on her .marriage to Sir Charles Maurice

Interior of The Manor's Dovecote c.2000

A PLAN
of the Manor of
PILTON PARK
in the County of
SOMERSET

The Pilton Park Estate c. 1800

36

Pole and it remained in Lady Pole's possession until it passed via her daughter into the Stuart family who sold it in 1875.

Since at least the times of Edward Rider the Manor House had been part of a large Estate known as The Manor of Pilton Park. A survey of 1771 shows the estate's division into four smaller units outside the Manor House itself; Hill Farm, Lodge Farm, Park Farm and Steanbow Farm. By the time of the first half of the 19th. Century the estate had been re-formed into three farms, Cumhill Farm; Park Farm and Steanbow Farm. The disappearance of Lodge Farm is only apparent since it had been incorporated into Park Farm. The total estate was measured as 747 acres in 1808, which had been formed out of The Deer Park and land formerly part of the Abbot's home farm. A plan of the estate around 1800 is shown overleaf.

Perridge House

We have already mentioned that by 1086 a piece of Pilton [2 hides worth or about 2-300 acres] had been detached and given to form part of another Manor. The detached part then became an element of the Manor of Alhampton, a few miles south east of Pilton, and now part of the Parish of Ditcheat .

The exact location of the area taken from Pilton was not identified in The Domesday Book, and to this day there are uncertainties about exactly where it was. In general terms however it is thought to be an area in the vicinity of Perridge House. The arguments for its location are however circumstantial, and it is hoped that further research will provide more conclusive evidence.

The early holders of the area are not in question. In 1086 it was held by Ralph Tortesmains [alias Ralph Crooked Hands], and his heirs continued as Lords until the late 12th./early13th. Century. By about 1250 the area had passed into the hands of Robert Fitz Payne and remained with this family until at least 1428 when the trail goes cold. However Glastonbury remained Overlords of the area until the monastic lands passed into the hands of the Crown in 1539 .

Later on in the early 18th. Century it was purchased by a Dr. Claver Morris. He was an interesting and active Physician of the late 17th, early 18th centuries.He married three times and it is said increased his wealth on each occasion. His main residence was in Wells but by 1710 had also acquired Perridge. At the time it was described as an estate consisting of six farms and residences, six barns, six stables six orchards, six gardens, and one dovecote. There was 74 acres of arable land, 52 acres of meadow, and a hundred and fourteen acres of pasture, making a total of 240 acres.

According to Phelps who wrote a history of Somerset, Dr. Claver Morris sold Perridge to the Burland family. However it is more likely that Mr. Burland obtained the estate by his marriage to Dr. Morris's daughter. Later it was sold to Stephen Stone of Bristol; who resold it to Partridge –Smith Esq., from whom it was purchased about 1800 by Major Thomas Clerk of the Honourable East India Company.

Today the house is a grade II listed building, described as a 17th. Century country house with gothic additions in the late 18th. Century .Further work is dated on a tablet at the rear "1909".

SECTION 9

===============LAND HOLDING============

Customary Tenants

From the earliest days of the Medieval period virtually all small landholders held their land according to the customs of the manor. When a tenant took over a tenancy only short details were recorded in the court rolls. Their name, money paid for the property, annual rent to be paid, land area, whether or not a Heriot would be due, and usually that was about all. In addition however there were a host of obligations and benefits attached to holding the property. These were usually covered by a phrase such as `......(the property is held) according to the customs of The Manor'. The earliest details we have for Pilton's customs is the result of an inquiry made in 1639, but they are based on customs going back to the early years of the Medieval Period.

The customary copyholder held property for the lives of three named persons. If a married tenant died leaving a wife she was due her widow's estate, which was one third of the property. If the Lord wished to sell a reversion/renewal he had to first offer it to the existing tenant, and when the tenancy fell into the Lord's hands it had to first be offered to the child of the copyholder or the next

kinsman before being offered to anyone else. Each time a tenant died a Heriot was due to the Lord consisting of the best goods of the tenant. The tenant could freely collect firewood from his own property and was allowed to cut wood for essential repairs. However he could forfeit his tenancy if he sold wood without the Lord's permission. He was obliged to use the Lord's Court for suing another person for amounts less than £10, otherwise he would risk forfeiting his property. He had common rights in Sedgemoor and Cramwell Moor for any number of cattle [but not sheep] at any time of the year. The tenants of Ham had extra common rights for cattle in the Forest of Mendip. Those of West Compton had rights of common on Green Knowle and also the right to collect firewood there.

For all tenants, rights of common for sheep were restricted to the common fields when they were fallow but only for three sheep per tenant.

Tenants were allowed to sub-let but only for a year, and for pasture not for tillage; any longer subletting without licence would entail forfeit of his property. Tenants had to report all wrong doings to the Lord or face a fine. Any animals which roamed loose in the Manor became the Lord's property and a fine had to be paid before they were returned. All tenants had to attend the Lord's Court and had to obey all orders made at it. All waste land was the Lord's property as were any goods of a convicted felon. If a tenant let his property decay he would be forced to make it good. If he was unable to do this, then his fellow tenants[i.e. those in the same tithing] had to make good. An interesting perk of customary tenants was to be exempt from paying market tolls within the County of Somerset. If a tenant was absent from his property for a year it was forfeited to the lord.

Whilst copyhold was the principal type of tenure these customs remained important. Gradually, however this type of tenure was replaced by the lease, and by the middle of the 19th. century most land and house holdings in Pilton were either leases or freehold. Interestingly as leases replaced the copyholds the tradition of making them for three lives was continued until the practice of making them for 99 years became standard .Many a 19th. Century lease also carried over the Medieval practice of paying Heriots. However by the 19th. Century the ' best beast' means of payment had been replaced by a money amount .

Enclosures

At the same time as the movement to leases, lands continued to be swapped and holdings became more compact and enclosed. The open fields reduced in size, and most of the common arable fields, pasture, and meadows had been encompassed into individual holdings by end of the 18th. Century. There was however need for one Parliamentary Enclosure Act relating to Pilton. It was passed

in 1796 and covered three different parts of Pilton.

One part was a few fields at Perridge Hill, west of Perridge Farm. This area consisted of 18 acres and 31 perch, which was split between Mr. Burland, William Gore, Mr. Hole, William Symes and Mr.Partridge-Smith. Westholme House was built. on part of this land.

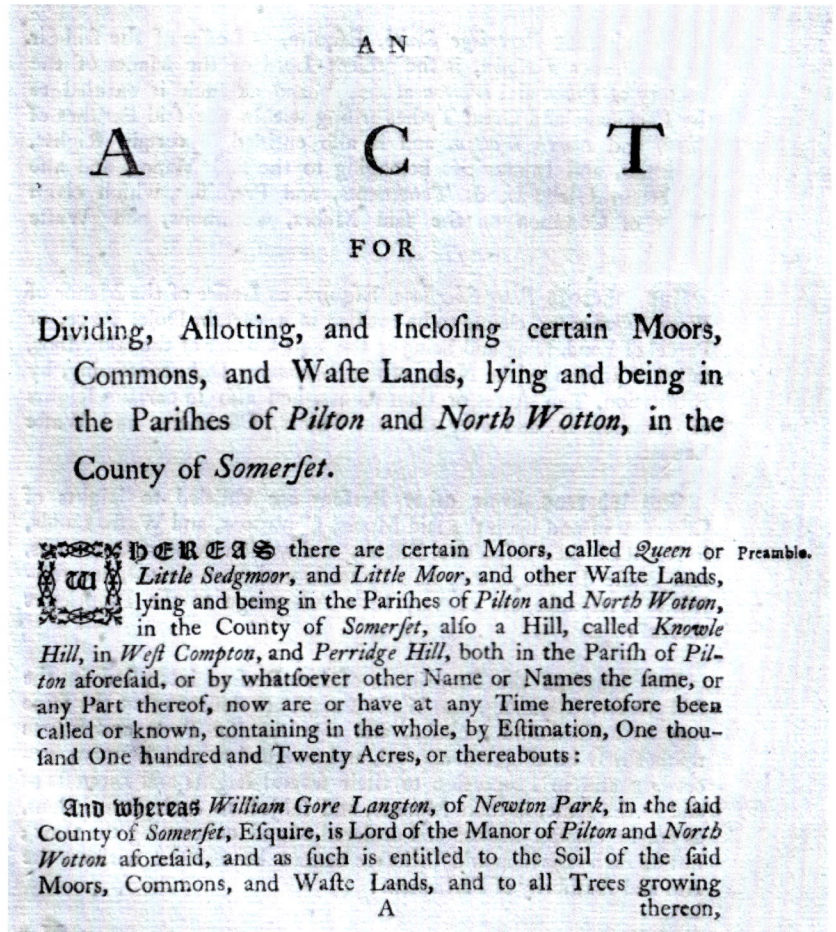

AN

ACT

FOR

Dividing, Allotting, and Incloſing certain Moors, Commons, and Waſte Lands, lying and being in the Pariſhes of *Pilton* and *North Wotton*, in the County of *Somerſet*.

Preamble.

WHEREAS there are certain Moors, called *Queen* or *Little Sedgmoor*, and *Little Moor*, and other Waſte Lands, lying and being in the Pariſhes of *Pilton* and *North Wotton*, in the County of *Somerſet*, alſo a Hill, called *Knowle Hill*, in *Weſt Compton*, and *Perridge Hill*, both in the Pariſh of *Pilton* aforeſaid, or by whatſoever other Name or Names the ſame, or any Part thereof, now are or have at any Time heretofore been called or known, containing in the whole, by Eſtimation, One thouſand One hundred and Twenty Acres, or thereabouts :

And whereas *William Gore Langton*, of *Newton Park*, in the ſaid County of *Somerſet*, Eſquire, is Lord of the Manor of *Pilton* and *North Wotton* aforeſaid, and as ſuch is entitled to the Soil of the ſaid Moors, Commons, and Waſte Lands, and to all Trees growing thereon,

A

First page of the 1796 Parliament Act allowing enclosure of Pilton's remaining common land

The second area was at Knowle Hill in West Compton [63 acres, 1 rod,7 perch]. Thirdly, a more extensive area was in Queens Sedgemoor in the far west of the Parish consisting of 879 acres 2 rods, and 32 perch, most of which was in North Wootton.

SECTION 10

================RELIGION================

A drawing of Pilton Church.(before 1839).

Religious Affairs

From the earliest of times the Church has played an important part in the everyday life of English Parishes. Indeed the word parish is itself based on the *parochia* of the Church which, is a specified area served by one church. Without a church there was no Parish. In Pilton's case the Parish and Manor were much the same area, but originally North Wootton was also considered part of Pilton Parish, as Wootton only had a chapel attached to Pilton as its mother church.

Christianity had probably reached Pilton by at least the late 6th. Century, but little is known about its religious affairs at this time. By the 7th. Century a Monastery at Glastonbury was established but it is unlikely that Pilton itself had a church this early. Often religious teaching took place in the open air. The next door Manor of East Pennard had an early Minster church, with Priests going out into the surrounding areas to preach. So perhaps priests from there used to venture

The Church and surrounding buildings c.1809

down the hill to Pilton to provide religious services. If a church did exist in Pilton before Norman times no trace of it is now visible.

For many years the Abbots of Glastonbury were at loggerheads with the Bishops of the Cathedral Church of Bath and Wells over who had control of the religious teaching in Glastonbury's Manors. The Monastery had great wealth and relatively light religious duties, and although the Bishops of Wells were not exactly poor they were spiritually responsible for the whole of Somerset. The disputes were frequent and often involved appeals to both the Pope and King. After one such dispute ending in 1174 the Abbey were forced to relinquish authority over Pilton church.

The handing over of responsibilities to the Cathedral Church was accompanied by the provision of a living for the priest. Part of the provision resulted in the vicar having special privileges in Pilton Park viz. the right to depasture with the Lord's cattle. eight oxen, five cows, one bull, and one plough-horse; 39 pigs free of pannage, and every day to have a burden of dead wood, and a block at Christmas and an allowance for eight men, and half a measure of oats for his horse and a penny to buy a halter. On the feast of St. Michael he was to have ten hens; on Ascension Day a cheese; and a bushel of corn against Easter.

He was also allowed an enclosure for a curtilage (or courtyard) situated adjacent to the Church on its north side. This enclosure was used to house the vicarage and barn, which remained in existence until the second half of the 19th. century when the Rev. Gray built the new vicarage. Also, along Parsons Batch close to the vicarage were tenements: the position of the buildings before they were demolished can be seen in the map opposite.

Tithes

An important part of Church income came from tithes. Dating back to the early days of Christianity , every landholder had to pay a tenth of his produce to the Church. For many centuries it was paid in kind but this caused difficulties, and in 1836 The Tithe Act was passed. This enabled monetary payments to replace produce in kind. A useful side- benefit of the Act was that all landowners were listed and their holdings mapped to a high degree of accuracy. In Pilton this was finalised by 1838. The area of the Parish was assessed at 5,470 acres of which 1046 was arable, 4,201 was meadow or pasture, and 130 acres of woodland. The great tithes were valued at £245. (see Appendix for further detail)

The Church

The church is thought to have been built in the early 1100's, but probably only parts of the wall of the main body of the church [the nave] and the base of the tower remains of the initial structure. In the 1160's the north wall was removed and replaced by the northern aisle and arcade. The lower level windows were built into the south wall in the 14th. Century. Between 1460 and 1470 the original walls were raised and the higher level windows inserted. By 1483 the roof had been replaced with the fine oak roof of today.

The eastern part of the church was added between 1480 and 1490, and the top part of the tower added in 1506.The addition of a south porch was completed by 1523 (restored C.19th).

In 1710 a gallery was erected at the western end of the Church to house the choir and orchestra, which in 1806 included a double base, a bassoon, a clarinet and flute. In 1852 the orchestra was disbanded and replaced by an organ. A second organ was donated in 1872, placed to the east of the south door.

The fine chandelier which hung in the Church until recently, was payment from the proceeds of a fine levied when a Pilton stocking maker, Mr. Hamwood, defrauded the revenue of duty on soap. It was customary in the 18th. Century that any information given to the tax authorities was rewarded with half the proceeds of the fine. It is said that Mr. Hamwood was so enraged that he never entered the church again. The chandelier was made in Bristol and is dated 1749 . It is hoped to soon rehang it.

In 1816 another gallery was said to have been built along the length of the north wall to provide 124 seats without pew rent i.e. for the poor. However this must have been soon altered as previous to the restoration in 1871, a plaque in front of the north wall gallery was inscribed as follows;

"The accommodation in this church was enlarged, and this gallery erected in the year 1825, by which means 112 additional sittings were obtained; and in consequence of a grant from the Society for Promoting the enlargement and Building of Churches and Chapels -76 of that number are hereby declared to be free and unappropiate for ever, and are in addition to 25 formerly provided.
H.W. Barnard, Vicar,
Thomas Phelps &
Robert Hoskins   Churchwardens"

Entrance to the gallery was above the north door with steps leading to it from the churchyard from both the east and west. There were also spiral steps at the west of the gallery inside the church. It only lasted about 30 years.

Another gallery was built around 1820 to accommodate the Clerk family. It was 12 feet long and 4 feet wide and positioned above the south door. This also didn't last too long and was taken down by Rev. Gray. Between 1841 and 1879 the Rev. Gray restored and cleaned up the whole church and by 1860 the galleries had been taken down and the walls freshly plastered.

Joseph of Arimathea

There is associated with Pilton church the legend that Joseph of Arimathea as a merchant made visits to Pilton , and that he brought Jesus [Joseph's nephew]with him on one of his trading missions. The claimed legend would seem to be based partly on an extension of the legend of Joseph visiting Glastonbury and also the belief that Pilton was a port 2000 years ago. The historian, Michael Costen, felt that on the basis of geological evidence alone Pilton could never have been a port at this time.(see appendix for further discussion).

Methodists

The Methodists had their roots in eighteenth century Anglicanism when a group at Oxford University met together during 1729-35 to discuss their religious ideas. They were nicknamed the Methodists because of the methodical way they pursued their faith. Led by John Wesley, an Anglican Minister, the movement prospered and by 1739 they had formed their first chapel in Bristol. At first they remained part of the Anglican Church but in 1780 they formally separated from it. An internal split in the movement occurred in 1808 with one fraction calling themselves the Primitive Methodists and the main group designated themselves as Wesleyan Methodists. Both these groups existed in Pilton, with The Wesleyan Methodists residing in Top Street. In 1932 they reformed with other Methodist groups to form the present Methodist church in Britain.

Methodist meetings in Pilton are said to date back to at least 1794, with Jubilee House (Top Street) as a meeting place. The existing Chapel was built in 1849, and opened for worship on the 4th. September of that year. It seated about 200 people, with a gallery for 40. Initially there existed two entrances to the Chapel's interior on either side

Methodist Chapel

43

, but they were abolished on account of the drafts they occasioned. Windows were substituted for the doors and a new doorway made in the centre. Extensive improvements were made in1883 when the Eastern Lobby was added. The chapel was amalgamated with the Ebenezer chapel in 1964.

Bible Christians

William Bryant a Cornishman and Wesleyan Methodist applied to become a Methodist preacher but was rejected. He broke away and formed his own ministry in 1815 together with James and John Thorne in Devon. The movement was initially known as the Bryanites but Bryant himself used the title of Minima Bible Christians, which was popularised as the Bible Christians by 1816.

The Ebenezer Chapel -. 2008

The building of the railways through Pilton brought many Cornish labourers to the Parish, a few of whom were Bible Christians. Some of these used to meet regularly at Church House for bible studies. Mrs. Allen herself a Cornish woman gave over a room for the purpose and built a separate entrance for them. Later they formed a local group of Bible Christians who took over The Ebenezer Chapel.

Initially the Ebenezer Chapel was built for the Primitive Methodists, who wanted every word in the bible to be taken literally and every Sabbath strictly observed. They built the Chapel in 1839 but their numbers declined and it was taken over by the Bible Christians in the 1880's

They in turn declined in numbers and the society closed down in the 1920's .

The chapel was taken over by the United Methodist Society in the 1930's becoming known as the Pylle Road Methodists Society. It closed in 1964 and the Chapel was sold in 1968 to become a private house. The last couple to be married there in 1962 still live in the village.

When first built the Chapel had a gallery and sittings for 120 people. It was 33ft. long 21ft.wide and its ceiling 18ft. high. A basement room was included in the building to serve as a school.

44

SECTION 11

===========CHURCHWARDENS=============

Early Churchwardens Accounts

Pilton has a good run of early Churchwardens' Accounts which have been published by The Somerset Record Society. They cover the years 1498 to 1530, and during this time the parish funds were administered by a single warden. He alone was responsible to the visiting church authority, and to the body of Pilton parishioners. Accountable to him there were, it would seem, four pairs of Wardens, viz., Our Lady Wardens, those of St. John's Brotherhood, those of the High Light on the rood-loft, and those of the Key (i.e. cows).

The Key Wardens are particularly interesting. They looked after the cows which had been gifted to the church. They either hired out the cows to farmers for a set fee, or sold the milk .When they hired out a cow , it would seem that a pledge had to be given to certify her good treatment.

1507..... a cowe the geft of John Brok p'ci (price) the cow –xjs. viij d. (11s.8d.) the hyre xxd. (20d.).
1508 ..... receved of Willyam Townysende and John Dore for Key Whyt ixs. vd (9s. 5d.).

(Willyam and John are thought to have been the Key wardens, and Key White the milk produced by the herd)

There were also two guilds associated with the church, that of St. John the Baptist, and that of The Hogglers. Both guilds were actively involved in fund raising for charitable causes, and donated regular sums to church funds.

> Little is known about the origins of Hogglers but they existed throughout Somerset. Their means of raising funds is thought to have involved visiting houses and providing entertainment and singing particularly at Christmas .

Generally the accounts show a steady flow of funds, and expenses seem to have been met without the need for special fund raising efforts or collections after services. A popular means of gifting to the church during this time was to donate small items of jewellery, mainly rings, or indeed any item of value. Some examples of these gifts are given below

1500......a grete brasse pott, of john Warde biqueste Item iiij (3) sponys of silver the gift of Walter Sargent.
1509........Item received for a peyr of bedes of the biqueste of John Hollere ys wyff
1516 .....Itm. A rynge of syller off the quest Annys Syppard with ij kerchows
1500........received of Isabel Hayne bequeste j rynge Item received of Margarate Coke ys bequest ij

45

rynges.

The total number of rings possessed by the church was considerable but as numbers varied from year to year some were probably sold to provide extra income when required.

1500.......The Some of Rynges in the ere of our Lord Gode mccccc xxli(31) and a crucifix.
1503 .....the sum off ryngs yn the streng amowntthyth to lxxxviij (88).............

Later Churchwardens Accounts

By the time of the 17th. Century there were two churchwardens elected ,one proposed by the vicar and one by the Parishioners. They held office jointly and no doubt helped and supported each other in a task which was getting more and more arduous as succeeding governments imposed additional duties upon them. It was also a sensible measure to inhibit any dishonest practices.

Upkeep of the Church structure was a continuing need thus;

1626...... pd. for glazing the Church windows.. . 9d.
Paid John Ridewood for tymber, nailes & work in
tymbering under the lead of the tower ...... 3s.
Pd.William Hurman for 57 lbs. of new lead
at 1 ½ d. the lb.   ..   7s. 1d.
For a day & half to him(Wm. Hurman) &
his sonne on top of the tower   ..   3s.

An expense item which was unexpectedly absent from the earlier accounts was that of Communion wine and bread. When this item did start being mentioned the amounts purchased would seem to be quite large. A total of forty one quarts and one pint was purchased in the year 1626. Similar amounts were purchased in other years, and perhaps the tradition of any left over going to the sexton may have influenced ordering.

1626   Pd. For 6 quarts of wine for the Communion
against Whitsuntide   6s.
For bread then   2d.
Pd. For 7 quarts of wine for the Communions
.......All Saints Day & the Sunday after   7s 0d
Pd for 10 quarts & a pint of wine for the
Communions at Christmas   10s.6d.
And for bread then   ....   2d.
Pd. For 18 quarts of wine for Palm Sunday,
Sheared Thursday,Easter Eve & Easter day   18s
Pd. For a bottle for the parish use to fetch
winein for the Communion   2s. 4d.

Upkeep of the church bells was a frequent item to be paid for. In 1626 there was only one mention, but in other years this expenditure was much greater.
1626 Pd. for two new bell ropes for the tenor &
second bell   6s.4d
1632....Pd. For mending of the 3rd. bell wheels   8d
For making a new Gudgeon for the 4th. bell
& for a new pynn for the wheels   2s. 6d.
Fore new keyes & a plate for the 3rd. bell   4d.
Pd ....for a new bell rope   3s.
Pd. The ringers the 5th. november   12d.

This ringing on Guy Fawkes Night was a yearly event for a number of years.

Travellers

Giving relief to travellers and vagrants was another payment which churchwardens were responsible for. This did not seem to be too big a problem in Pilton as the amounts given were relatively small. In 1626 nine travellers who passed through the village were given aid., and similar numbers occurred in other years. Mostly the recipients of aid were war pensioners , but in some years there were many poor Irish travellers seeking relief.

1626........Given a poor traveylor with a pass   2d.
Another poore man coming out of Turkey   2d.
Item given to a poor man coming out of captivity
out of the Low Coutries .   2d.
To a souldier commin out of Angyer   2d.

Briefs

During the seventeenth and eighteenth centuries there was an increase in the popularity of 'briefs'. These were royal or ecclesiastical mandates for collections towards some deserving cause. It was a national scheme and at times so common they represented ' This week's good cause'. The brief was supposedly read out in church and the congregation asked to make a contribution. In Pilton however it would seem that they were paid for out of the moneys handled by the churchwardens, and often the Vicar paid a sum which he thought was appropriate and was afterwards reimbursed by the churchwardens .

1626...........Given unto two briefs laid out by
Mr. Abbott [vicar] afore 16 of Julie   *12d.*
Given to a brief to one John Walker for
£800 loss at sea......in this countrie   *6d.*
given to a brief for a church in Dorsettshire   *7d.*

Briefs were widespread throughout the country and the practice lasted for a number of centuries. However over the years they were associated with several scandals .It was also often the case that the administrative costs of collecting them became so high that there was little surplus to distribute to the deserving charity. They had died out in most areas by the 19th. Century.

Miscellaneous

Another interesting insight into past centuries is that a Curfew bell was still being rung in Pilton in 1637.The ringing of the church bell to announce curfew was a leftover of Medieval regulations The bell was rung at a set time , after which all fires were supposed to be damped or extinguished for the night.
1637.......Pd. Anthonie Fortune his yearly wages for keeping the clocke and ringing of Curfue   *10s.*

There were at least two organs being used in Pilton church during the 17th. Century,and a man was employed to provide the air. It is interesting that the wage for this activity did not increase for at least eleven years, and that probably the same family formed the service during this time.

1626...... John Copp, his yeares stipend for keeping out the dogs & blowing the Organs   *6s. 8d.*
1637....Pd. Peter Copp the Sextyn his years wages keeping out of Doggs, keeping clere the church and blowing the organs   *6s. 8d.*

It was not unusual in the 17th. Century for dogs to accompany their owners to church, and it was the job of a subordinate of the wardens to keep them in order.

Another duty imposed on the wardens was to provide a net for the capture and destruction of various birds. This duty had the force of statute from 1532 onwards. Parishioners were paid a set fee for their captures usually a few pence per dozen birds. In 1632 Anthony Thompson was paid for killing and keeping out stares[i.e. starlings] and other birds from the church. The accounts show that his fee included the cost of powder for his gun. There were also set rates for destroyng hedgehogs, foxes, and other vermin, all paid for by the churchwardens.

Also it is interesting to note that in 1785 the accounts refer to the disturbances caused by the playing of balls against the Church wall.To stop the nuisance it was found neccessary to dig up the ground around the church . The game causing the nuisance is not described in detail but it was probably a variant of fives , which was very popular at the times.

SECTION 12

================TRANSPORT===============

Roads

Originally the liability for maintenance of the highways lay upon the holders of the land. The first road act upon the statute book -the Statute of Winchester of 1285 – clearly recognises the local Manor's responsibilities in road repair. For over two hundred years therefore road upkeep was clearly the responsibility of the manor through which the road passed. Not that the Lord himself took responsibility, as he would cast this obligation onto his tenants and enforced it through his Manor Court.

At the same time as the authority of Manor Courts declined the volume of inter manorial trade increased, resulting in a deteriorating condition of the roads.There were various piecemeal measures adopted in the reign of Henry VIII and in that of Philip and Mary. Finally in 1555 a Highway Act was passed which remained the foundation of highway law for nearly three centuries. By this act the Manorial duty was transferred more to the administrative body rapidly growing in favour with the central authorities, the Parish. The new leglislation specified that able parishioner had to provide both equipment and labour for four days a year in repairing the roads.The number of days was increased to six by later Elizaberhan leglislation. The supervision of this unpaid 'Statute Labour' was entrusted to the Surveyor of Highways (also unpaid). In Pilton each tithing had their seperate surveyors and they became reponsible for the roads in their own area. However there were often difficulties in getting this labour to turn out and on occasions money was raised through the rates to hire paid labour.

August25th. 1831
At a vestry meeting held this Day pursuant to a Notice given on Sunday last immediately after Divine Service. It was ordered that a Rate of sixpence in the pound in lieu of Statute labour,be made and collected by the Surveyors of the Pilton Tithing
James Bethell   Charles Orledge   Wm. Orledge Robt. Orledge   John Griffin

If the roads were not maintained to a satisfactory standard the Parish could be fined. These fines could be quite substantial. For example in December 1831 Pilton was fined £100 by the local justices for not maintaining the road in the far west of the Parish near the Redlake River. This road was in the area of the tything of Westholme and Holt. There was some debate on whether this tything should pay all of the fine but eventually it was agreed to spread it around all the five tythings of the Parish. Further details are given in the appendix.

Turnpike Trusts

An agricultural community such as Pilton was largely self sufficient and except for the occasional trip to market there was little need to travel. When they did travel it was not neccessary to do so speedily. As commerce expanded however, greater pressure was put on the roads and they became less and less able to cope with the increased traffic. This applied particularly between large towns, with a special problem along important routes where the traffic using them and causing wear and tear of the roads had little to do with the local Parish it was travellingt through. Not suprisingly such Parishes were loath to expend much on road maintenance.

After the English Army got bogged down while marching north to Scotland, Parliament decreed that something had to be done. They didnt want to raise taxes so they passed leglislation enabling local trusts to be set up to provide money for road repair. The means was by charging each road user a toll, and allowing the Trusts to borrow whenever required. This meant placing a gate across the roads and users had to pay a toll every time they passed through. Usually a house for the gatekeeper was built adjoining the gate In practice The Trusts didnt operate the gates themselves but auctioned off the tollgates annually to the highest bidder, who then set the tarriff and collected the money. The gates varied trmendously in value. Thus Shepton Mallet Trust's gate north to Bristol and Bath was worth £802 in 1819 compared to only £71 for the Pilton gate west of the town leading to

glastonbury.

Between 1752 and 1759 Trusts blossomed throughout Somerset. The most important from Pilton's point of view was the Shepton Mallet Trust which was set up in 1753. Amongst the roads under its jurisdiction was the Glastonbury - Shepton road [now the A361 and B3136]. The Pilton stretctch was turnpiked in 1753. At Steanbow was a main toll gate; a second gate was installed in 1803 across the road to North Wootton. The other main gate was situated at the V-junction where the A361 is met by the B3136. The Trust continued in business until 1878.

The other company operating through Pilton was The Wells Turnpike Trust, which operated two routes going through The Parish. One ran from Wells to Dulcote and continued along the Old Wells Road , then continued

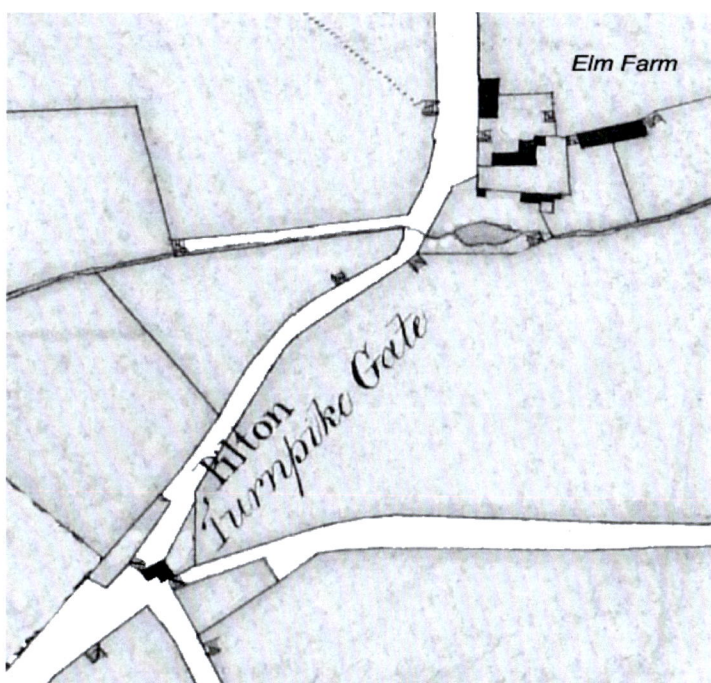

The 1809 map shows the position of the gates and toll keepers cottage at the V-junction

WELLS TURNPIKE.

A Ticket from this Gate will Free the next Gate you pass through on the Wells Trust.

TABLE OF TOLLS.

	s.	d.
For every Horse or Beast, drawing any Coach, Barouche, Sociable, Berlin, Chariot, Landau, Chaise, Calash, Curricle, Chair. Phæton, Caravan, Taxed Cart, Hearse, Litter or other such light Carriage, (except Stage Coaches,)	0	4½
For every Horse or Beast, drawing any Stage Coach,..............................	0	4½
For every Horse or Beast, drawing any Caravan, Tilted Waggon, Tilted Cart or other such Carriage, carrying Passengers for hire, ...	0	4½
For every Horse or Beast, drawing any Waggon, Wain, Cart, or other such Carriage, having the Fellies of the Wheels thereof of less breadth than four and half Inches at the Bottom or Soles thereof, ...	0	4½
For every Horse or Beast, drawing any Waggon, Wain, Cart, or other such Carriage having the Fellies of the Wheels thereof of the breadth of four and half Inches, and less than Six Inches, at the Bottom or Soles thereof,........	0	3½
For every Horse or Beast, drawing any Waggon, Wain, Cart, or other such Carriage having the Fellies of the Wheels thereof of the breadth of six Inches at the Bottom or Soles thereof, ...	0	3
For every Horse, Mule or Ass, not drawing	0	1
For every Drove of Oxen, or other Neat Cattle, per Score, (and so in proportion for any greater or less number),..	0	5
For every Drove of Calves, Swine, Hogs, Sheep or Lambs, per Score, (and so in proportion for any greater or less number)	0	2½
For every empty Coach, Chaise, Waggon, or Wain, Cart or Dray, or other similar Carriage drawn at the Tail of any Waggon, Cart, Dray or other Carriage....	0	9

For every Coach, Chariot, Chaise, Chair, Cart or other Carriage, affixed or drawn at the Tail of any Waggon, Cart, Dray or other Carriage, having any Articles or Goods conveyed therein, other than the Harness thereto belonging and such Articles of Package as may be necessary for the protection of such Carriage—*Double* the Toll, otherwise chargeable upon the Horse or Horses drawing such Carriages.

For every Stage Coach or other Public Carriage, having more Passengers than the same is Licensed to carry, or having a greater weight of Luggage upon the top of the same than is authorised by Law, or having Passengers riding on the top of such luggage,—*Double* the Toll, otherwise chargeable upon the Horses drawing such Coach or other Carriage.

Tolls to be paid for or in respect of Stage Coaches, and other such Public Carriages, or for the Horse or Horses drawing the same, (except Post Chaises and other Carriages drawn by any Horse or Horses travelling for hire, under the Post-Horse Duties Acts,) every time of Passing and Re-passing ; and also for Post Chaises and other Carriages drawn by any Horse or Horses travelling for hire, under the Post-Horse Duties Acts, or for such Horse or Horses, upon every new hiring.

N.B.—Two Oxen or other Neat Cattle, with respect to the payment of Tolls, when drawing, to be considered as one Horse.

☞ The several and respective Privileges and Exemptions, granted and allowed in and by the General Turnpike Act and the Wells Turnpike Act, are allowed here.

BACKHOUSE, PRINTER AND BINDER, WELLS,

A table of tolls for the Southovre Gate,(c.1825) similar tolls applied at all Wells Turnpike Gates

through the northern parts of Pilton, along The Ridgeway, and on to Canards Grave .It was turnpiked in 1764 but disturnpiked by 1821. The other route operated by The Wells Trust was an unlikely one from Wells to North Wootton and then southwards through Pilton and Lower Westholme to Steanbow before going up Stickleball Lane and continuing to Parbrook. It continued on to Langport and Somerton, with a branch to Castle Cary.The relevance of the route was due to the fact that both Wells and Somerton were assizes towns, necessitating much traffic between them. The route was turnpiked in 1764 and disturnpiked in 1821.

> The table of tolls on the previous page was posted on all Wells turnpike gates in the early 19th. century. Note the lower prices for vehicles with wider wheels. This was because the wider wheeled vehicles resulted in less damage to the road surface.

The tolls were much disliked by everyone, especially the locals who had to pay for every sheep they took to market; alternative routes were often looked for.One such route involved cutting across the fields before Steanbow towards Worthy Farm, up the hill to the top of Mount Pleasant, along the bridleway to East Town continuing on the bridleway to East Compton,and then north to Shepton thereby, avoiding two sets of tolls.

Stage Coaches

In conjunction with the improvement of roads came the Stage coach era. This gradually evolved from the 17th.century onwards and by the 18th. centuries most major towns . had at least one Stage coach compay operating services though it. Pilton at the time, not being on a heavily used major route had no regular services, and locals had to travel to Wells , Shepton , or Cannards Grave before they could pick up a service. For eample in 1767 you could pick up a Poste Chaise service at the George Inn Shepton Mallet. This ran every Sunday,Tuesday, and Thursday at six fifteen in the evening and carried parcels and people to Frome which linked with a full coach " The One Day Flying Machine " which reached London 16 hours later. The cost was twenty seven shillings, and by comparison an overnight stop in a decent inn cost three shillings and six pence, dinner two shillings, and breakfast one shilling.

Increasingly in the late 18th. and early 19th. centuries passengers and mail travelled in the same coach. In some areas this had commenced shortly after 1750 but the earliest found local mail coach service was in 1836. This came from Wells via the Old Road to Shepton Mallet then to Devizes and thence on to London.

Tthe coach services were mainly for the better off, but also operating at the same time were stage wagons.These were much more numerous than stage coaches and much slower. They were mainly for goods but also accepted passengers, and as they were cheaper were the usual method of travelling for the poorer people who were unable to walk long distances. It wasnt until the coming of the railways that the poorer classes could afford faster travel.

Railways

The main line railway network reached Somerset in June 1841 when the line from Bristol was extended to Bridgwater. A further extensions to Exeter being made by 1844. For the next 25 years lines were springing up throughout the County.

By the 3rd. February 1862 there was a line

through Pilton . This was an extension of the Highbridge to Glastonbury line which had existed since 1854. It continued first to Cole and then onto Templecombe. The line was initially built for The Somerset Central Railway Company who in 1862 joined forces with The Dorset Central Railway Company to form The Somerset & Dorset Railway (S&D), often known as The Slow & Dirty. The line went through the southern part of the Parish , but there were no stops in Pilton itself. The nearest station for most residents ws at West Pennard (about 200 yards beyond The Apple Tree Inn

alongside the A.361) . The line closed in 1966.

A second line went through Pilton in the extreme North of the Parish. Built as an extension of The East Somerset Railway Company line from Shepton Mallet to Wells in 1862. Again there was no station in Pilton and the nearest for most residents was Shepton Mallet Town Station. The line was closed in 1963.

Both lines are marked on the map of Pilton at the front of the book, whilst the extent of the rail network in Somerset is shown below.

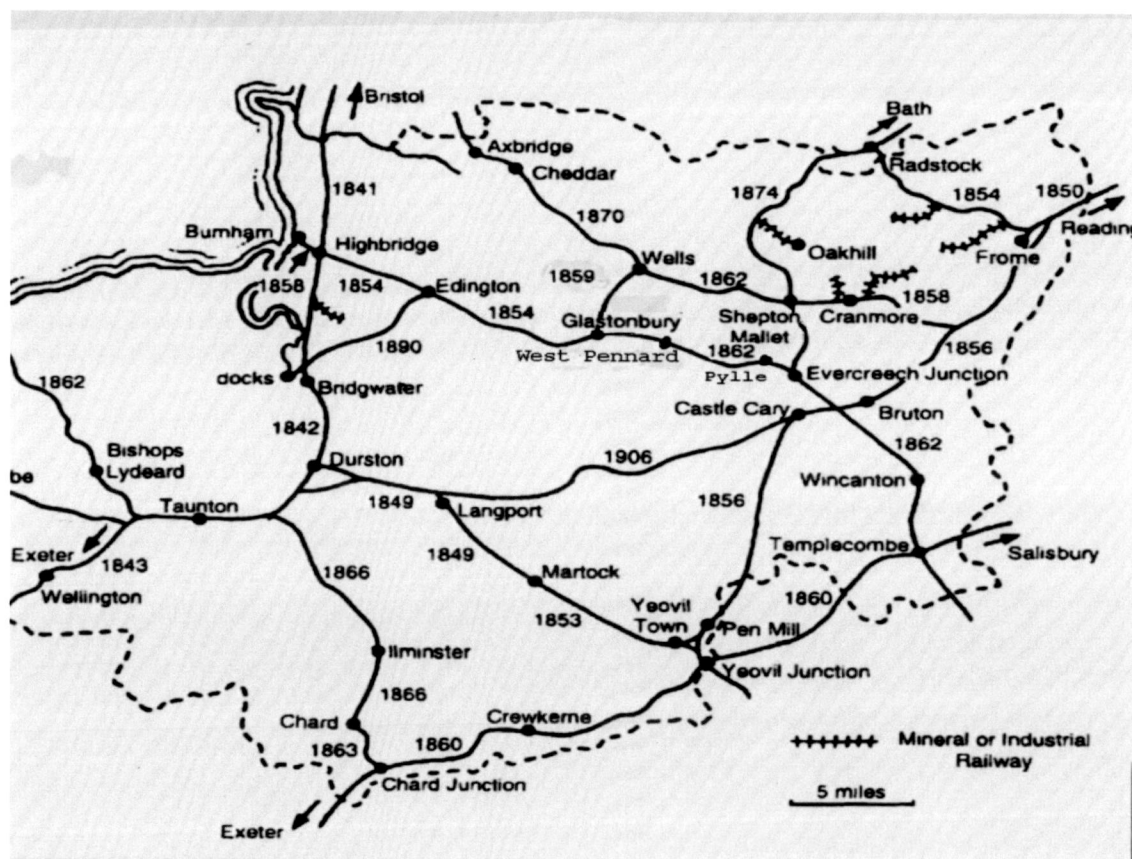

Somerset Rail Routes (with years of opening)

SECTION 13

===============EDUCATION===============

English educational ideas had been gradually developing and expanding over many centuries. By the beginning of the 19th. Century, schooling of one type or other had penetrated to more than half of the population. In Somerset alone there were over 900 various types of schools (virtually all fee paying) by 1818. However much of the educational instruction was centred around the bible and included Sunday schools. Often the length of schooling was as little as a year. There was much resistance to extending education to all social groups and many a Parliamentarian believed that it was for the best that poor people were not educated above their station. Nevertheless the movement for a more general education continued ,and from 1833 the government started to provide grants for school buildings.

Until the late 1840's there was no general schooling available in Pilton apart from the privately run `Dame Schools'. This situation

The School Playground before it closed- 1968

53

started to change on the 2nd. March 1846. The parish vicar the Rev. H.F. Gray conveyed a piece of land to himself as vicar and the churchwardens of Pilton for a school under an Act passed in 1841/2 entitled " An Act to afford further facilities for the conveyance and endowment of sites for schools"

The land involved was already owned by the church and known as " Home Field". It was 25 perch in size and to be `....used for a school for the education of poor persons of and in the Parish of Pilton, and as a residence for the master or mistress of such school and no other purposes. The said

early starting age continued to at least the 1890's..

In 1870 the Elementary Education Act made it compulsory for all children aged 5-13 to attend school. This increased the number of pupils and a second classroom was needed. £80 was raised to build one. By 1890 there were 200 pupils in the school with three teachers.

The dimensions of the two classrooms were 50 ft. 5 inches long by 17 ft. 5inches wide, for the older pupils' room; and 32ft. 5in. long by 16

The Junior school c. 1925

school shall always be in union with and conducted upon the principles and in furtherance of the ends and designs of the Incorporated National Society for promoting the education of the poor in the principles of the Established Church.' The school was able to accommodate 150 children and supported and built by voluntary contributions.

In the early days pupils paid 1d. per week which had risen to 2d. by 1895 after which attendance was completely free. The school took pupils from as early as 3 years old and this

ft wide for the infants, both rooms having fifteen foot ceilings. There was a small playground, of eleven yards by fifteen yards, and two small cloakrooms of eight and 9 square feet. The toilets were outside; and from the mid 1920's the boys used the garden next to the village hall for gardening lesson, while the girls did needlework.

The number of pupils in 1902 was recorded as varying between 71-74 for the senior school, and 42 -55 for the infants school The average for the year was 122 which was a typical

54

number for the early years of the 20th. Century. There were three teachers for the older school, and two other assistants for the infants. The headmaster in 1902 was Horace Henry Corsbie and his wife Mary headed the infants section.

The senior curriculum in 1902 consisted of, English, Arithmetic, Geography, History, Drawing (boys), Needlework (girls), Object lessons (common things) ,Singing by note, Physical training, Military Drill. At the end of the school year there were 90 books available for the senior school and the Board of Education's Report said of the senior section that it was "a capitally organised and well taught school"

Religious studies are not mentioned as part of the main curriculum as it had its own inspector who was sent to the school by the Church authorities.

The infants subjects consisted of the three-R's, reading writing and arithmetic, needlework(both boys & girls), Drawing (boys & girls), simple lessons on common things, and

appropriate varied occupations, singing, and physical execises .There were 60 books available for the pupils, and the Board of Education Report assessment was "The infants classes are taught with very fair success".

The total cost of the school in 1902 was £266, of which grants from the Board of Education amounted to £188, leaving £79 to be raised by local means. The headmaster was paid £98 p.a., the infants' mistress £50, and other junior teachers £40 or less.

From 1927 the school ceased to teach pupils over 11 years, and most continued their secondary education in Shepton Mallet. By 1956 the school was down to 58 children, 28 infants and 30 juniors. Despite opposition from local people Somerset Council amalgamated the school with West Pennard and it closed in 1969.
(A detailed memory of the school in the 1890's is included in the Appendix)

The Senior School c. 1917

55

SECTION 14

==========CIVIL AFFAIRS=============

Civil Administration

We have already noted that the origins of the word 'Parish' is an Ecclesiastical one. For Pilton the Ecclesiastical Parish started when the Established Church took over Pilton Church from The Benedictine Monks in 1174. At that time Manorial authority was the stronger and a greater influence in Pilton's day-to-day affairs than the Church. Gradually however as the Feudal system faded the church became more and more important in the civil administration, and national Acts of Parliament continually added to their responsibilities.

One of the earliest acts was in 1538 when the priest was made responsible for registering baptisms, marriages and burials. The Civil Parish started to become distinct from the Ecclesiastical one when Poor Law defined the Parish as a place which levied a separate rate. The institution of Pilton as a civil parish was completed in 1894 by the formation of Parish Councils.

The Poor

The tradition of a parish supporting its poor was a firmly established principle from as far back as Saxon times. All support had to come from local efforts, either the family and neighbours, the Lord of the Manor, or the Church. There was no national scheme of assistance. Statutes had been passed as early as the 14th.century reserving a part of the church tithes to be distributed to the poor. However it was often thought that too much charity could deaden the sense of personal responsibility and make matters worse.

> The 1494 Beggars Act determined that. "...... Vagabonds, idle and suspected persons, shall be set in the stocks for 3 days and 3 nights and have no other sustenance but bread and water and then put out of town.....".

Some harsher Statutes from the 16th. Century onwards specified penalties for those who gave private alms, and it became illegal to beg and roam around the countryside. Vagrants had to remain where they were and if it wasn't their place of birth they were to be forcibly sent back to their birth place. Later, scales of penalties were introduced for those deemed able to work, ranging from whipping for the first offence to loss of ears for the second and hanging for the third.

Another atrocious measure in 1547 imposed branding and slavery as the punishment for persistent vagrancy. However intermingled with such harsh legislation were more humane ones such as enforcing the gathering of voluntary alms every Sunday with boxes in church specifically for the poor. Parsons also had imposed upon them the legal duty of exhorting his parishioners to show charity to their neighbours. Exhortation and voluntary alms were seldom enough and in 1601 Queen Elizabeth introduced her great Poor Law Act .This Act was initially intended as a temporary measure but it was to become the very foundation of local poor-law administration for over two centuries.

Early accounts about poor relief in Pilton either have not survived or are virtually illegible, and not until the 19th. Century is detailed information available. By 1777 Pilton had set up its own Work/Poor House (now the Parish Hall), there being places available for 30 people.

By 1835 large numbers of people were getting some form of poor relief in Pilton. For example in just 2months (April/May) 94 different people are mentioned as receiving relief, spread across 65 different families. The amount spent was £101- 12s.-8d., a yearly rate of over £600.

Many of those who received relief did so on a regular basis ,with payments of three to four shillings a week being typical amounts for the basic necessities of living :food, fuel rent and

clothing etc..(an example of a full month's accounts for April 1835 is given in the Appendix).

> Regular weekly payments in 1835 varied widely from five pence a week up to just over six shillings, with an average of three to four shillings per person.

The overseers would also pay for specific items, usually articles of clothing, and on December 15th. 1831.....

At a Vestry held this day it is agreed to allow the poor as follows
William Lambert a coat.
James Williams a pair of shoes
James Carpenter some hessian for a bed tie
Patience Bryant a petticoat
Some bedding etc. for the Hoarse children
Ann Jacob a shift.......
(more details are given in the appendix).

The money spent by the overseers was entirely raised by rates on Pilton's householders. Thus in 1832 a poor rate of 9 pence in the pound was levied for maintaining the poor[vestry minutes] The exact amount paid by each householder depended on the rateable value of the property, but generally varied between several shillings for the smaller houses to tens of pounds for the larger properties.

> In 1831 Elizabeth Sims looked after the poor house. She was paid 4d. a day for washing and cleaning for the poor people , and generally doing what was needed to be done.

One way of reducing the continual drain on Parish funds accounted by the poor was to encourage them to emigrate. To achieve this end there are a number of instances in the

Vestry minutes in the 1830's where parishioners were given financial assistance to emigrate .Thus on April 24th. 1832:

.................at a Vestry meeting held this day it was agreed to pay the sum of fifteen pounds and no more towards paying the expenses of Robert Andrews, his wife and family to America.

Possibly this assisted emigration caused some concern amongst parishioners about whether the money would be properly spent. Thus later the same year on October 4th. 1832:

......at a Vestry pursuant to regular notice it is agreed to advance ten pounds to William Martin to enable him, his wife and family to go to America, on Martins Father giving proper security to the parish to see them go.

Charles Orledge   churchwarden
Richard Jeffery   overseer
William Orledge
Francis Hamwood
Robert Orledge

Settlement and Removal

Until 1662 the poor could seek employment wherever it might be found., but after that date legislation made it more and more difficult to take to the road in order to look for work. For the poor, the Parish became a virtual prison. A poor man could only travel outside of his home parish if he had a certificate from an official agreeing to take him back if he became too poor to support himself. If he did obtain work elsewhere and resettled but later lost his job he could be forcibly moved back to his home Parish. It could be   particularly harsh on women who lost their husbands.

> Females changed their legal settlement on marriage, adopting their husband's legal place of settlement. If a girl married a man in her own parish and he died she would automatically be removed to her husband's along with any children.

There were complicated rules defining the settlement Parish but they were open to interpretation. Frequently legal wrangling took place between the two Parishes involved, spending much needed money on lawyers rather than on the poor themselves.

At a vestry held this day (July 4th. 1844) pursuant to notice given on Sunday last to determine the course the overseers are to adopt with regard to an order for removal of Hazel Beale and her two bastard children from the Parish of Shepton Mallet into this the said Parish of Pilton !In was resolved that the overseers be authorised to apply to Mr. Phipps to give notice of appeal to the churchwardens and overseers of the Parish of Shepton Mallet and to obtain councils opinion on the case.
H.F.Gray (chairman)

There was much ferrying of people and children between Parishes . Usually this was reasonably local as people did not venture far from their home Parishes. Sometimes however longer distances would be involve for example in 1835 a journey from Leicester was necessary. The settlement problem continued to be an important issue late into the 19th. Century

On 3rd. January 1743 Edward Spinlock (about 18 years of age) was removed from West Pennard to Pilton.

An order dated 2nd. January 1745 lead to Sarah Masey and her seven children being removed from Pilton to Woolavington.

Harry Brown, Mary his wife and Henry ,William, John, Mary ,and Gertrude their children were ordered to be removed from North Wootton to Pilton on 10th. Jan 1745.

Work Unions

1834 legislation set up Work Unions and out relief was discouraged. So any poor requiring relief from the Parish had to go and live in the Work House . A few years later Pilton became part of The Shepton Mallet Union with its Work House in Shepton (later to become The Norah Fry Hospital). Pilton ratepayers contributed their share to the Unions 's funding but the more detailed attention to individuals became the responsibility of the Work House. rather than the Parish. The administration of the Poor Laws gradually was taken out of the hands of local bodies and by 1918 mostly transferred to the Ministry of Health

Law and order

Originally the responsibility for local policing was a manorial one with justice being mainly given out in the Manor courts and for more serious crimes The Hundred Court.. The tithing man or Constable was an important part of the process both at the Manor and Hundred courts. His position goes back to the 12th. century ,and he was usually appointed at the Manor Court. Gradually over the years however these responsibilities were altered by National Legislation and devolved onto the vestry and the churchwardens.

Reported first in The Sun 3rd. Dec. 1793. Thomas Withy was taken into custody for murdering his estranged wife who had been found in a nearby pond in Pilton. He admitted the offence and was hung on 31st. March 1794.

By the early 1840's there were reputed to have been 17 beer and cider shops in the Parish and there was much drunkenness. To help counteract this the village appointed its first policeman in 1842. Joseph Duncan was the first constable at a wage of £15 a year but he was not given a truncheon until 1844.He resigned in 1845

In March 10th. 1847 John Selway was appointed constable for a wage of £10 a year, His duties are recorded in the Vestry minutes as follows:

Memorandum of the duties which the paid Constable for the Parish of Pilton will be expected to discharge for the salary of ten pounds
To serve all Warrants for the whole parish of Pilton. To attend the Magistrates meetings at Shepton Mallet and Wells, when there is business for the Parish to be transacted. To take care that the provisions of the Act for regulation of the Beer and Cider Houses be obeyed, and to give information when they are broken. To attend to disorderly persons on the Sunday, and generally to discharge the duties specified in the Act

To which John Selway gave signed agreement.

In 1856 the County Police Force was formed and took over the duties of the Parish Constable in the same year.

SECTION 15

=======AROUND THE VILLAGE===========

In order to bring out some of the interesting historical aspects of the village we invite you to a walk around Pilton. The walk is largely based on one first described in the History Group's publication of 1988 "A Walk Through Pilton's Past"

We start at the Village Hall [1-on the map overleaf].This was much renovated and added to as part of an improvement programme commencing in 2005.However the front of the building , which faces onto St. Mary's Lane, was left largely unaltered The building originally on the site is thought to have been a guest house for Glastonbury Abbey (commissioned by Adam Sodbury who was Abbot of Glastonbury 1322-35). After the Dissolution of the Monasteries it was used as a Church House where church fund raising activities took place, often accompanied by the consumption of ale and entertainment. Such events known as Church Ales were a frequent method of raising money for the Church. There is record of an Ale held there in 1592 raising nine pounds towards funds. The

building is referred to in the Church Wardens' accounts of 1511 as needing a new roof, it took 100 bundles of straw to thatch it. At that time it was known as 'Saynte Mary's House'. Later a ceiling was put in and the space partitioned to make individual rooms and it became the Poor House of the Parish. At one time as many as ten poor families were housed there and this use continued until the 1830's when the Shepton Poor House Union was set up. By the 1890's it was in a ruinous state of repair (being used as a stable and pigsty by a local farmer) and was bought by a local benefactor, Edmund Clerk from Burford. He demolished the old

The Village Hall

60

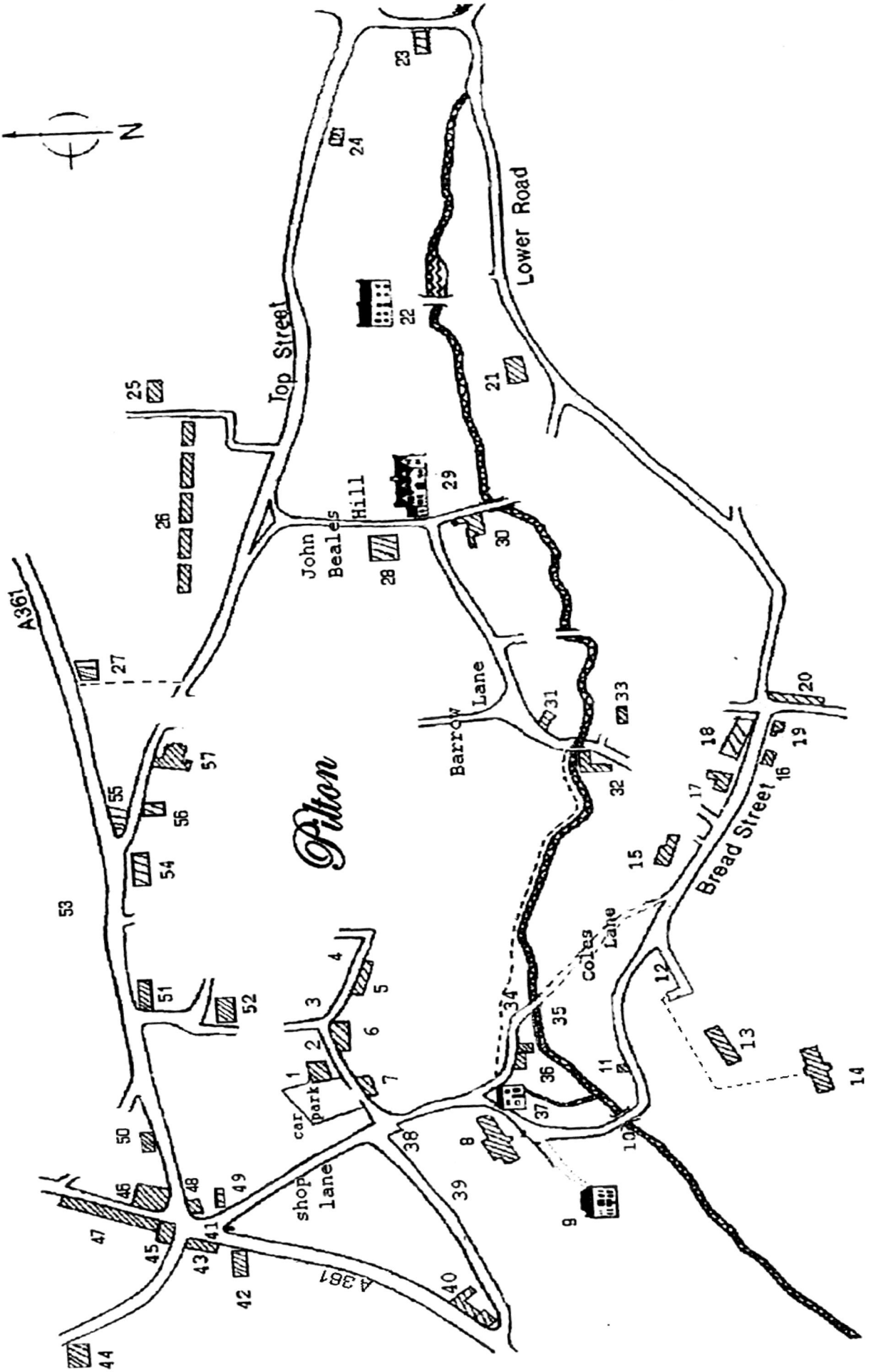

N

A361

Top Street

Lower Road

John Beales Hill

Pilton

Barrow Lane

Coles Lane

Bread Street

A361

car park

shop lane

Cottage formerly on the site of Spring Cottage [3] c. 1910

Further along [4] once stood Barrow Stile Inn, now a modern bungalow. Its license was squashed around 1912 and the building demolished in 1920. Rodgers the butchers once owned the Inn and it is said used to display the meat on the tops of beer barrels. Entertainment was provided by Isaak (Ike) Webb who played jigs. A customer who complained about the music had Ike's fiddle broken over his head! Jack Carter was the last landlord.

On the other side of the lane is Barrow Stile Cottage[5] which is about 300 years old, the eastern part of the house was a small shop [1890-1920's]. The western wing appears to be an old stable and the adjoining outhouse was once a slaughter house.

building and then rebuilt it as closely as possible to the original structural plan retaining only the cellar of the original building [now used as a Youth Club].He presented it to the Parish in 1893 for use by the working men of the parish as reading and recreation rooms.

Next to the Hall on the site of No.1 Abbots Way [2] there used to be The Full Moon Inn. In the 1930's it was occupied by Mrs. Burridge and the back part used as a bakery by the landlord, Thomas Cary. It can be seen opposite Church House in the 1938 photograph. The building was demolished in the 1950's to make way for the Abbots Way bungalows.

Opposite [3] is the relatively modern house, now called Spring Cottage but previously on this site was an attractive thatched cottage[.see picture above].Known as St. Mary's Cottage, this also served as a bakery for a few years

The funeral of F. Slade 1938 showing the bier cart. The Full Moon Inn (now demolished) can be seen next to the Parish Rooms.

Returning back along St. Mary's Lane we come to Church House [6], formerly Church View Farm. This is a 16th. Century building and probably built in Queen Elizabeth's time when stone started to replace the wattle houses of the time. On a pane of glass in a window there is scratched "William Middle 1619 his act and pen" From church registers we know the Middles were active in Pilton in the 17th. Century. Later Elizabeth Strode an heiress of the wealthy Strode family of Ham House in Pilton was living there. She was courted by Amos Allen whom she married. There is a local story that no sooner had he taken possession of her fortune than he took her to Shepton and put her up for sale. A kindly Pilton farmer is said to have seen her plight, paid the necessary fee and brought her back to Pilton! In the 18th and 19th. century the stocking trade for the Spanish market was an important source of home income for Pilton and many other villages in the area. At one time a third storey had been added to the house but in 1923 it was found to be too heavy for its foundations and removed. Found in the attic were "dozens" of woollen stockings hanging from the roof. For many years in the 1890's John Allen ran a general stores there and Mrs. Allen ran a sweetshop.

Next door is a building built before 1500 and called St. Mary's Cottage [7] since the 1960's, but previously known as Cum Hill View. Up to 1890 it was also known as The Hole in the Wall Inn

Back view of St. Mary's Cottage

because drinks were served through the window. Probably at that time the road was at a lower level. The house originally was a hall and service room with a chamber above it. The room facing west is a seventeenth century addition but the roof timbers date from an earlier time. An unusual feature is that its well was inside the cottage. In the mid 19th. century the building used to be two cottages.

Pilton Church c. 1869

Turning left down Shop Lane we pass the church [8] on the right [see section 10 for additional details]; this beautiful building has been much altered since it was first built in the 11th. Century. We include a photograph of it taken around 1869, looking north. Note the then newly built vicarage on the skyline behind the church. The old one was still standing at the time and its thatch roof can be seen in the photo between the church roof and the new Vicarage.

The Manor House c.1905

When the old Vicarage was pulled down the ground was added to the churchyard (consecrated 1898). Some of the older residents have left stories that at one funeral a coffin fell through the ground into the old vicarage's cellars.

If we continue along we reach The Manor House. [9].This was originally built by Michael of Amesbury [Abbot of Glastonbury 1235-52] but only the cellar of this period has survived. It was a favoured summer residence of many of the Abbots partly because of its large adjoining Deer Park. It was handsomely remodelled in the 18th. century when the present frontage was added .It has an unusual plan with two halls at right angles to each other, a layout found in only two other Somerset buildings. It was the base for Pilton vineyard

which was re-established in 1966 and at its peak produced some 40,000 bottles of wine per year; it closed in 1999. The original vineyard dates back to at least 1189 and is mentioned in a survey of the Manor of that date. For many years there were extensive buildings in front of the Manor House, just to the south of where the entrance gate now is there was a lodge. [See section 8 for additional details]

The road continues across the stream as a bridge [10] but which is perhaps as much a causeway. Notice how the Manor's walls from the gate onwards slope downwards before levelling out. This is because originally the road sloped right down to stream level but is now built up 15 feet or so above the stream. This was done by Mr. Broad in the mid 1800's in order to reduce the steepness of the road up Cumhill to Bread Street. Mr. Broad, who kept The Swan and brewed beer, made the improvements for the convenience of his brewing carts when carting malt from Bread Street to his brewery up on the main road. The original low level bridge is believed to be the one mentioned as being crossed by Abbot Beere in his perambulation of the 12 hides in 1503 and known then as "Burybrigge"

Cumhill farm c1920

South face of The Abbey Barn, probably pre-1940. The roof before 1963 was mainly thatched and edged with stone tiles as in the photo.

A little way up Cumhill on the left is what looks like an isolated garage but is in fact a Bier House [11].This was used to store the burial cart between burials [see photograph of F. Slade's funeral]. Both the burial cart and building was given to the Parish in 1910 by Hugh Dobson of Perridge. Next door is a modern house but in the 19th and 20th Centuries the site contained a row of small tenements, housing four different families.

At the top is the start of Bread Street, where if you turn sharp right the single house on the right [12] once was the site of two small thatched farm cottages, Cumhill Cottages, before they became condemned and pulled down shortly after the Second World War. Continue along the footpath and on the left is Cumhill Farmhouse [13]. This attractive building dates back to at least the 16th. Century and has in its time served as yet another Inn. It has smoked blackened roof timbers suggesting a past which included a medieval hall and hearth. Although now a private residence, for most of its history it was a farmhouse for Cumhill Farm which was part of The Pilton Park Estate [see section 8]. Its antiquity, and its closeness to the Abbey Barn,

and Manor House makes it an obvious candidate as the farmhouse of The Abbot's Home Farm in medieval times.

Continuing along the footpath brings us to the magnificent medieval barn locally known as " The Tithe Barn" [14].In fact it was built by the Abbey for their own use and never owned by the church. (The Vicar had his own barn next to his vicarage) It is unlikely therefore to ever have been a tithe barn in the usual sense of the term. The precise date of building is unknown but from its architectural details and comparisons with other Glastonbury barns it was probably built at some time in the 14th.century. Its internal dimensions are 108 feet long and 28 feet wide and is the largest of the surviving Glastonbury Abbey barns. Others are at Doulting, Mells, West Bradley, and Glastonbury [part of the Rural Life Museum]. It most resembles the Glastonbury one and their similarities in workmanship and design leave little doubt they were both built by the same craftsmen. One of the most distinguishing features of the barn is its carvings. The emblems of the four Evangelists being on the gable ends, viz.the Lion of Judah (St. Mathew), the Good Man (St. Mark), the Sacrificial Ox (St. Luke) and the Eagle (St. John) It is a somewhat two-faced barn in so far as its north face [the one which would have been seen by the Abbots from the Manor House] has ventilation provided by ornamented cross slits. [Cruciform openings] whereas the south face has just simple slits. The original roof was probably of stone tiles, later it was thatched and then destroyed by lightning and fire in 1963. Since 2003 its roof timbers have been re-built as close to the original as possible and the roof re -covered with clay tiles. The building is now in the hands of a specially formed charitable trust.

The Symbol of St. John – The Winged Eagle on the west gable.

Doorway to Malta House

Retracing our steps to the beginning of Bread Street and continuing eastwards we soon come to Malta House on the left. [15]This is a 15th. Century maltster's house. It is worth paying attention to its particularly fine doorways; a handsome 18th. Century stone doorway to Little Malta, and an earlier semi-depressed, four centre stone doorway to Malta House. The building was originally an open hall house with three rooms - it still has its smoke blackened roof timbers. Until the 1950's there was a bakery immediately behind Malta House: George Mullins was the last baker there and in the 1870's the ovens were used as malting kilns. A school was at one time kept in the most eastern Malta cottage, a Dame school run by Mullins' daughters charging fees of 2d. per week for 20-30 pupils. Little Malta was the home of David Cornwall and his wife before he became well known as John Le Carre.

Further along we reach the top of Ford Lane. Here stood one of the village's gravity fed water pumps, the other being at the corner of Bread St. and Watery Lane at Cornerswell. Along Bread Street on the right is Arch Villa [16] which in the 1890's was the home of the village police station. On the left is 17th. Century Mulberry Cottage [17] which was two residences until the late 1970's- Nestor House and Double House [the latter itself being originally two houses]. The well at Double House was one of only three that did not dry up during the great drought of 1921-the others being at The Dell and Weavers Bridge.

Further along on the left is a row of attractive 18th century cottages [18] the end one [Cornerswell] still has its' well visible in the front garden.

Immediately opposite is Vicars Cottage [19] so called as it was left to the vicar by "Witch Andrews". Across the road is The Long House [20], built by a shoemaker called Chambers from West Pennard on waste ground in the early 19th century. The site was originally very narrow so it was built long and tall. It was never the traditional long house of previous centuries which were built to house animals at one end and humans at the other. At one time it was called Long Wheat House. George Binning baked bread there 100 years ago. Later, corn grinding was carried out by the Cambells, and a shop selling everything from poultry food to groceries, the shop remained in existence until 1971.when it became a Hotel. It has now been split into two residences. The pulley once used to haul up sacks of produce can still be seen.

If you were to continue past the Long House along Pylle road, you would shortly

Bread Street looking east

reach the turn off to Worthy Farm (home of The Pop Festival). Further along Pylle Road on the left is the early 19th. Century Orchard House (another ex- pub).

A few yards along on the right is the Ebenezer Chapel, now a private residence, but still with its gravestones in the front garden. Built in 1839 for the Primitive Methodists it closed as a chapel in 1968 (see also section 10).

Another half mile or so along Pylle road just beyond the edge of the village is The Bush. This was built to accommodate workers when the railway was being built through the Parish and was known as The Bush Inn. It remained functioning as a pub until the 1950's and is now a private home and nursery.

Returning to the end of Bread Street; Climb up Mount Pleasant and at the top is a group of 18th. Century cottages, keep your eyes open and you will see on the right by the roadside a covered up well

Descending the hill into Lower Road [previously known as Valley Road] we reach Gable House [21] on the left. Owned by the stocking maker Mr. Hamwood in the 1790's, his fine for avoiding duty on soap paid for the church chandelier. The doorway is of late Tudor date as are four similar fireplaces inside the house. The house was formerly part of Pilton House estate.

The Long House

Further along on the left is the attractive Pilton House [22]. Built in the time of Charles I [1625-49] for a family called Hole.

Pilton House

Continuing along Lower Road we come to Yew Tree House [23] on the bend. It has a sundial on its south wall dated 1786 and is another place which has served as a shop in the past, first as a butchers run by The Gould family then later as a general grocers run by Mrs, Srickland until the 1980's.

The road at the crossroads to the right is East town Lane and you may wish to take a short diversion along it. Shortly on the right is Wellands, a house which has a date stone "1664", although the buildings have late 18th. century alterations. Also worth visiting along the lane is Riverdale and East Town Farmhouse. Both houses at one time were attached to mills and Riverdale probably dates back to medieval times. All three houses are listed grade two. East Town House had a stray bomb dropped into the yard during the Second World War which resulted in serious damage to the house.

There was no male heir and a daughter of the family married a Welshman named Bethel. The house then remained in continuous ownership of this family until 1980 when it was sold at auction. There were no title deeds to the property and a marriage settlement from Victorian times was taken as proof of title. The doorway contains the inscription "I.H" and the date of 1629. Close inspection shows that the doorway is not centrally placed and the layout suggests adaptation of the building to the fashionable regular look of the 18th. Century. Although the stairs are now in a later extension, the original winder stairway can be traced in the attic in the traditional location. Next to them is a typical 17th. Century moulded wooden door frame. The two windows to the left of the door are in the original service room and it is not impossible that the house started as a long house with animals and humans using one entrance to access the separate parts of the building.

Grey Gables

Return to the crossroads and continue along Top Street; Beechcroft [24] on the left is a cottage which was once a private school run by Miss Trevelyan.

A few hundred yards along on the right is Culverwell Passage and here, in the field below Culverwell House [25], is Hangman's Close. In 1890 whilst quarrying stone here to build Culverwell House a mass grave was discovered which was excavated by Bath Archaeological Society. The skeletons had crossed arms signifying death in conflict but otherwise it is not known whether the conflict was the Civil War or The Monmouth Rebellion.

Next along Top Street are Culverwell Cottages, [26] the first 12 being built in 1938 on the allotment field for those made homeless by condemned housing in other parts of the village. If you continue along Top Street, on the right is a footpath leading up to the main road. At the top of the path you come to Walnut House [27] where Tapper Norris had his cobbler's workshop in the garden, and up to the 1920's his wife ran a haberdashery shop from the house.

Returning back down the footpath, retrace your route along Top Street and turn down John Beales Hill. Cedar House on the right. [28] was the base of the Boy Scouts between the wars, and in the 19th. century was occupied by the John Beale who gave his name to the hill.

Almost opposite on the left is the thatched house known as Grey Gables [29]. The dormer windows were installed in 1637 and are handsome examples of building

Beales House

improvements of the period. Grey Gables together with the house opposite, Beales House [30] were both originally open hall houses as evidenced by their smoke blackened roof timbers, and date from the 15th. century with rebuilding in the early 17th. Beales House (known as The Ferns in the 1930's) was once split into three residences. Just below Grey Gables was a stocking factory and along with Beales House, Wellands in East Town, Gable House [Lofty Lodge] and Church House formed the centre of the stocking industry in Pilton, the stream water being used for washing.

Lancet Window in the wall of Burrow House

69

Barrow House & Ford

the area up Pylle Road which once contained a large pond.

Take the picturesque footpath along the stream. Half way along is a weir and the path then continues very straight to the gates of Monks Mill [37].This was the route of the leat stream powering the waterwheel of the mill. The leat continued in existence until into the early 1900's At the back of the mill down the steps into the garden was an annexe used as an edge tool works in the 19th. century.

Turn towards Barrow Lane and soon on the left is the late 17th. Century Barrow Cottage [31]. Continuing down to the ford, as you cross the footbridge you will see Barrow House on the right.[32]Notice the small lancet window set low to your right known locally as the "Lepers Window", which probably originated elsewhere. The house was once two dwellings with a footpath going between them [claimed as a right of way up to 1927]. Once a busy farmhouse with a large dairy to the left of the house it has largely been restored from a ruin in the last 40-50 years. We are now in Ford Lane [commonly known as Fear Lane] and across the lane is Old Worthy [29] which was previously known as The Gardens. The house has a large Tudor doorway set in a square headed frame. The footpath that went through Barrow House also went through Old Worthy. Before crossing back, notice the conduit coming out in the road just south of the stream; this drains

Monks Mill in the foreground. (View from the Church Tower c.1920)

View at the bottom of Coles Lane across the stream. The row of cottages on the left is now demolished. Notice the thatched roof of Whiteleaf Cottage.

The Domesday Book mentions two mills in Pilton and it is thought that one of them may have been at Monks Mill. Today it is a private residence and only its name gives any indication of the previous mills existence.

Near Weir Cottage there used to be a small cottage, Mill Cottage. [34] Here Sid Stevens, a grave digger lived in the 1920's.The cottage is now demolished and on its site stands a modern garage. His cottage can be seen in the photo of Monks Mill, its the second building down in the top left corner. Just across the bridge [35] was a row of four cottages (pulled down in 1938) which instead of gates had a stile in an attempt to keep out any floodwater. They can be seen also in the Monks Mill photograph.

The path leading up to Bread Street is called Coles Lane, and used to be the 'main road' before Cumhill's gradient was "flattened".

However we shall head back up Weir Lane towards the church passing the 17th. Century Whiteleaf Cottage [36] on the left. This is attached to The Dell, a cottage dating from the 18th. century but having 15th.century origins. It had a wing added to its central room and contains a plaque " 1731 D.L.H. " The Dell itself was once owned by the Dunkerton's, the last being George Dunkerton, a bachelor. When George died he left the property to his four surviving sisters. In 1888 it was sold at auction to John Hambledon Beale, mason, who owned it until he died in 1936. He is said to have spent much of his retirement in the stable(now a garage) smoking his pipe and talking to his horse. The Dell had apple and nut trees, a pigsty, hen-house, and masses of soft fruit. Mrs Dell made 150lbs of jam a year

The Dell

71

The village stores & Pub in Conduit Square c.1920

and the family was largely self sufficient. There was a wonderful well in the yard and an old pump with a large wooden handle in the wash house, the water was said to be very soft and was never known to have failed.

Proceeding up Shop Lane to the cross road with St. Mary's Lane and Parsons Batch, just outside the church gates [The Bond Memorial Gates] was the site of the village stocks[38] . There is record of them being re-newed in 1799 and they were perhaps the same ones ` used' by the last man to be placed in them, a certain Job Sage, for beating his wife. Turning up Parsons Batch notice to the left the Church wall [39] which can be seen to be still partly formed by the end of one of the cottages demolished in the 1860's. Further up on the right is The School House and The Old School now private residences.[see Section 13 for more detail on the school]

Crossing over the main road, take the footpath going right alongside the main road. The field on your left was called Stoneyfields and a cannon ball has been found there. The field is said to contain graves of men who had fought at the Battle of Sedgemoor during the Monmouth Rebellion in 1685.

Continue up to the crossroads called Conduit Square [41], because of an old drainage system under the road. It was once known as Chauville's or Shawswell Cross.

A stream runs under Toll Cottage[43] and comes out south-east of the former Post Office opposite before going underground at the corner of The Working Men's Club car park and re-emerging at Monks Mill. Before reaching Conduit Square on the left you would have passed The Smithy, the site of Pilton's last blacksmith, also it housed a wheelwright. Next along on the left is a small cottage known as Toll Cottage [43].Despite its name it was never a turnpike toll house but at different times served as a carpenters shop and a Dame school.

Outside the Old Brewery c. 1890.

Around the corner along the N. Wootton road is Hartley House[44] which at one time was yet another baker, -run by the Binnings family who occupied the house from the 1890's to 1951. The oven there was capable of baking up to 300 loaves at a time and was able

Rodger Butchers c 1910 (former Post Office)

to serve the whole village.

Returning to Conduit Square is the Pilton Stores and Off- Licence [45]. Until 1898 this was The White Swan Hotel, with The Crown Inn [46] used as a lodging house for coachmen and as a drinking place known as The Tap. It was here that Monmouth and some of his men are said to have rested in June 1685 before their vain attempt to take Bristol.

In the early years of the 20th. century Augustus George Williams [the store's owner] had not only the first car and motorbikes in Pilton but an acetylene gas plant which lit Pilton Stores.

The owners of the Swan [The Gloynes} branched out and started a brewery in 1860 which used to occupy the buildings [47] along Totterdown Lane. At eye level, above one of the doors is a large stone with the year 1865 carved on it.. The brewery remained in business until the 1890's and was sold to Walter R. Baxter in 1893. Later for a short while it was used for cider making. Until 1994 Bill Appleby lived and worked in the building at the far end. He was one of the last traditional wheelwright and craftsman in the village. Today the buildings are occupied as a private house and sculptress studio.

Opposite is the former Post Office [48] (closed in 2007), which in turn was formerly a butchers (closed in 1979). Once a bakery with its ovens in the yard at the back, it is now a private residence. It is worth noting that a sub post office of Shepton has existed in Pilton since 1843.

On the corner of Shop Lane there used to be the Village Pound where stray animals were impounded by the Waywarden and only released on payment of a fine. The war memorial monument opposite was put up in 1920. A few yards down Shop Lane on the left is a small cottage, The Cot[49], which in its history served as a smithy and the shop from which the lane got its name. Continuing eastwards along the main road, look out on the left for Clematis Cottage [50] dating from 1624, and further along on the right is Yew Tree Cottage [51] dating back to at least. the 1500's. It has had much rebuilding over the centuries and there is a date on the fireplace lintel " I.D. (Isaac Dunkerton) 1684".In the early 1900's it

The Garage attached to Wesley House

The Old Bakery & Park View in Top Street

was two residences and in later years has served as a doctors surgery, and a bed and breakfast establishment for cycling clubs. The stair well was built around a tree trunk, and a workshop at the end of the garden housed one of the village blacksmiths in the 1830's.

Just down the hill is Shutwell House [52] which at times was a bakery and up to 1939 a furniture work shop. Beside the house used to be a pond from which a stream ran down the hill. The pond was fed by a spring that also fed the gravity fed water pipes to the rest of the village. The spring still bubbles up and runs between the road and the garden before going underground beside the Abbots Way bungalows and village hall and ending up in the stream at Monks Mill. Going back to the main road continue eastwards until you get to the start of Top Street. On your left across the main road is the Fair Field which used to be used for the annual fair, which had been held there in early September since before 1861.Later, in the 1890's, flower shows started there which became locally popular and entries used to be received from many of the surrounding Parishes.

On the corner is The Old Bakery [54] which has had various lives, as an antique shop, a laundry, a bakery, and in the distant past an Ale house. Opposite is Wesley House [55] which was attached to a garage operating until 1988. It had 2 petrol pumps. Previously for many years it had repaired and sold bicycles, charged batteries for radios as well as repairing them in the days of valve radio. For 25 years or so the owner Ted Gould ran regular coach excursions from the garage. Both The Old Bakery and Wesley house have their own wells; the latter's being inside the building.

Further along Top Street is Jubilee House. [56] There is a plaque dated 1887 on its east wall at first floor level, but it was known to have housed the first Wesley Chapel meetings which had started at least by 1794. The window openings of the north facing ground floor are different styles to those of the first floor. Possibly the plaque refers to rebuilding when the first floor was added or altered. Further along on the right is the present Methodist Church [57] which was the Wesleyan chapel until 1964 when it combined with The Ebenezer Chapel. It first opened for worship in September 1849, with the vestibule added in 1883 following a gift from Mr. William Orledge of West Compton. [see section10 for additional details]

This bring us to the end of our walk, but there are many other buildings of historical significance in other parts of The Parish. Of particular interest are the Red House and Knowle Farm in the far north west of The Parish, both showing evidence of dating back to Medieval times. A record of the listed buildings of Pilton is included in the appendix.

APPENDIX

Included in this appendix are references, additional notes for each section, and indications for further reading. The order of the contents here is generally the same as that in the body of the book. Often there is additional information which may be of interest for those wishing to go into more detail. Abbreviations used for the references are; S.R.O. - Somerset Record Office at Taunton (the letters and numbers following are their catalogue reference) ; P.V.H.G. stands for Pilton Village History Group whose archives are in the Village Hall; S.R.S. are publications by the Somerset Record Society which are available at many Somerset Libraries. Monetary amounts are always pre-decimalisation , i.e. 240 pennies (d.)=20 shillings (s)= 1 pound (£)

Section 1

1. The main books consulted for information in this section are
a) " Somerset " by Shirley Toulson
b)" The Archaeology of Britain " Ed. J. Hunter & I. Ralston
c)" The Archaeology of Somerset Ed. Michael Aston & I Burrow
d)" Prehistory of the Somerset Levels" J & B Coles
2. Information on early man's presence in Pilton is contained in P.V.H.G. D/231/2,
3. Further information on the evidence of Neolithic roundhouse findings is in an article on the University of Birmingham's excavations at Cannards Grave(PRN 44779) in the Somerset Historic Environment Web site .

Section 2

1. A useful book on The Romans is " Roman Somerset" by Peter Leach
2. Our thanks are to Sue Boone for uncovering and identifying the Roman and Saxon pottery finds in the Parish
3. The interpretation of the origins of Pilton's name is based on a" Dictionary of English Place-Names" by A.D. Mills. In the Dictionary he quotes the earliest known spelling of the name as *Piltune* in 725 ,and *Piltone* 1086 (Domesday),and interpreted it ' as a farmstead by the stream'. Stephen Robinson in his book" Somerset Place Names" , gives it only a slightly different emphasis i. e. ' the creek enclosure' , and both say it is based on the old English *pwyl*-or *pyll*- ,meaning a (non- tidal) creek or stream . Margaret Gelling a respected authority on the origins of place name also supports this explanation of its origins but mentions the possibility that the component *pyl*- could be derived from the Celtic word *wyl*. The second part '–ton,' is also Old English and comes from- *tun*, meaning an enclosure farm or smallholding.
4. A detailed analysis of the Anglo Saxon Charters can be found in" Anglo- Saxon Glastonbury, Church and Endowment" by Lesley Abrams. In the book he mentions that the bounds of Pilton in the Charters are expressed in words which suggest an origin of the late 10th. Century at the earliest and may be as late as the 13th. Century rather than the 8th. Century claimed by the Monks. He also points out that one of the charters includes Pilton as a church which is specifically excluded by King Ine as coming under the jurisdiction of the Wells Bishops. This was a blatant forgery as King Ine had died some 200 years before The Wells Bishops were established.
5. "Domesday Book"-Somerset, edited by Caroline & Frank Thorn is the book used for information about Pilton's Domesday entry. The italicised portion below corresponds to the translation of the Latin extract given in the text.
' *The Church holds PILTON itself. Before 1066 it paid tax for 20 hides. Land for 30 ploughs. Besides this the Abbot has land there for 20 ploughs, which has never paid tax. In lordship 10 ploughs;15 slaves; 21 villagers and 42 smallholders with 10 ploughs on the land which does not pay tax. 2mills which pay* 10s; meadow,46 acres;pasture40 acres; woodland 1 league long and ½ league wide. 4 cobs;35cattle;56pigs;500 sheep; 42 goats. Of the land which does not pay tax Alnoth the monk holds 1 hide freely from the Abbot with the King's assent. It was thegn land; it cannot be separated from the church. Value of whole £24; the value was £16 Roger of Courseulles holds 6 ½ hides of the manors land (i. e. Piton's) in Shepton and 3 hides in Croscombe. Wulfred and Aelmer held them before 1066; they could not be separated from the Church. In lordship 3 ploughs ; 8 slaves;13 villagers and 19 smallhoders with 6 ploughs. 2 mills which pay 6s. 3d.; meadow, 50 acres, underwood 42 acres; pasture 3 furlongs long and 1 furlong wide. Value of whole £9Also of this Manor's land Edred holds 5 hides in (North)

Wootton from the Abbot. Serlo of Burcy 5 hides in Pylle and Ralph Crooked Hands holds 2 hides in Pilton itself. The holders before 1066 could not be separated from the church. In Lordship 4 1/2 ploughs; 8 slaves; 8 villagers and 8 smallholders with 3 ploughs.,2 mills which pay 4s. 6d.,meadow 36 ½ acres; pasture 20 acres; woodland 4 acres. Value of whole £ 7-10s. between them.'
(nd.additional information given in the Exon Domesday shows that the 2 hides of Ralphs land contained 1 plough in Lordship , 1 smallholder,2 slaves. 1 cob,4 acres of meadow, and was worth 30s. in 1086 and 40s. in 1066.)
6.Other books consulted include " Domesday England" by H. C. Darby , and " Domesday Book, A Reassessment" Ed. P.Sawyer.

Section 3

1.The illustration of Medieval Peasants ploughing is taken from the Luttrell Psalter 1320-40 in The British Library.(as are the other similar illustrations in the next 2 sections) .The Plough is thought to be typical of what was being used in Pilton during these times, though the number of oxen used to pull it was greater (six or eight).The dress of the agricultural workers would have been typical for Pilton in the 14th. Century.
2.The most useful books on Medieval England consulted were;
a)" The English Manor c. 1200- c. 1500" Ed. Mark Bailey
b)" Life On The English Manor" H.S. Bennett
c)" The Medieval Economy and Society" M.M. Postan
d)" Life in a Medieval Village" F. & J. Gies
3.The map showing remnants of open field strips is part of the earliest known map of all Pilton . The complete map can be found at S.R.O. DD\SAS/C549/1
4.Information on agriculture in Pilton can be found in " The Granger of Glastonbury Abbey" by I. Keil, and also his unpublished Phd. Thesis available from Bristol University. In this thesis he notes that in Pilton one bushel of wheat per acre was sown, and two bushels per acre for barley.
5.The short extracted copy of Pilton's Court Rolls for 1304-5 is from S.R.O . T\PH\Ion/2/23/10778. The latin of the photographed extract roughly translates as;
"Pilton. The Hallemot for the term of St. Michaels(29th. Sept to Christmas) held Wednesday in the feast of Pope Saint Calixti(14th. Oct)In the year of Abbott........ the second....
Robert Redhol(fined 6d). for trespass in the Moor,Geoffrey Garland.(6d.). Walter Brounyng (6d.), William Brouning (12d)........at Barewe (Barrow), (6d), Adam Tornepeny (6d) for the same Thomas Le Daubour (3d) for 2 bullocks in the meadow, John Le Ban (3d) for 2 cows, John Le zonge (2d) for 1 ox, William de Bordecombe (2d) for 2 cows, Richard Elys (3d) for 2 oxen, Christine Ryde (3d) for 2 bullocks. Walter Faber (4d) for 6 oxen, Richard at the More (3d)for 2 cows, Adam at Sonde (2d) for 2 cows, John pohan(3d) for......".
6. Other extracts for the Manor Courts are; for 1262 T\PH\Ion/2/23/10682; for 1265 T\PH\Ion/2/23/10683; for 1283 T\PH\Ion/2/23/11250.There are over 50 entries for various Pilton courts listed at the record office , they are microfilmed copies from the originals kept at Longleat Library.
7.A detailed analysis of the Easter Court Polls is available in "Exploitation of the landless by Lords and Tenants in the Early Middle Ages by H.S.A.Fox (an article in the book " Medieval Society & the Manor Court")
8.The boundary of the Glastonbury XII hides was walked by Abbot Bere between the years 1503-10, a translation of the section of the perambulation relating to Pilton is given below , the walk approaches Pilton Park from East Pennard. Land to the west of the boundary was in the Glastonbury XII hides and to the east The Whitestone Hundred. Translation of the original is by S. Rand and Grundy.
'..............(and beyond the west corner of William Colbourne's meadow) as far as the stile standing in the fence of Pilton Park called the stile of Bechenhams well, where we were met by the homage of Pilton, down through the middle of Pilton Park to Hardelondebrygge thence to Selysdore[over the Whitelake] and the boundary between Shepegrove and Dorvale as far as Noddewey and thus from the south side of the old dovecote to the abbots Barton, thence through the middle of the Abbots orchard and thus by Burybrgge to the stone called Mere Stone that stands before the Abbots door, and the first days progress ended. The second days progress began at the Mere Stone in Pilton churchyard and it entered the church by the South door and went out by the North door; up through the graveyard and out between the vicars houses and the orchard thus uphill north to Ayshwellcross (probably Burford Cross)then north west to Chowellecros by the road or path that leads to Wotton, thus directly to Westelleygate thence to the broad road to Wotton.............'
9.Further details of the relationship between The Glastonbury XII Hides and The Whitestone Hundred can be found in " Glastonbury 12 Hides " by S. Morland S.A. N. H. S. 1984 9 v.128)

10.Collinson in his 1796 "Antiquities of Somerset " lists the number of houses in the four tithings as 1) Pilton 140 houses, 2) E& W. Compton 40 houses, 3) Ham 22 houses, 4) West Holm & Holt 20 houses. The population comprising a total of 1200 souls.

Section 4

1.The Henry de Sully survey and some explanation of terms can be found in "Surveys of the Estates of Glastonbury Abbey c. 1135-1201" Ed. N.E. Stacy.

2.The illustration of Peasants harrowing is from the Luttrell Psalter(c.1330), as is the peasant threshing.

3.The survey of Abbot Ford can be found in S.R.S. No. 5 "Custumaria of Glastonbury Abbey, 12th. Cent."

4.In addition to the two surveys discussed there is also in the S.R.O. a copy of the 1317 survey by Abbot Fromond . However a translation has not been found., although it is known that the survey lists for Pilton 10 free tenants, 10 tenants for life and 162 customary tenants. Another survey c. 1500 by Abbot Bere suggests that by this time work services had largely disappeared..

5.The Reeves accounts for 1330/1 are to be found at S.R.O.ref. T\PH\Ion/2/18/10761 ;for 1274/5 T\PH\Ion/2/14/11244

6.The part of the first line of the 1330/1 accounts given in the text reads Pultone, Compotus Walteride Hynebrigge p(re)positi……….which translates as; Pilton. The accounts of Walter Hynebridge, reeve……

Section 5

1.General books which have been consulted for the background on Medieval Parks are;
a) " Somerset Parks & Gardens" J. Bond
b)" The Medieval Parks of England " L.M. Cantor
c)" The Forests & Deer Parks of Somerset " W. Cresswell.

2.The 1227 court case involving the Park can be found in S.R.S Feet of Fines(1196- 1307) – Vol6.

3.Details of the different Manors who helped build and maintain the park are given below. The information is contained in Abbot Fords' 1260 survey published by S.R.S. The first name for each Manor is as it appears in the survey, the second (in brackets) being the present day spelling. A conversion factor of 16 feet to one perch has been used as this was the standard length of a perch in Glastonbury Manors of the time. (note, the original manuscript contains an error of 20 perch in one of the entries)

"Customary service given in Pilton Park and the villages which must enclose it"

Dultinga (Doulting) must begin from the dovecote facing Pennard and must enclose………

	perch	feet
....	120	(1920)
Melnes (Mells) afterwards...70	"	(1120 ")
Batecumba (Batcombe)...50	"	(800 ")
Dichesgata (Ditcheat)...100	"	(1600 ")
Pennard 80	"	(1280 ")
Baltonesbergh '(Baltonsborough).............................50	"	(800 ")
Wrington..120	"	(1920 ")
Brentmares (Brent)..140	"	(2240 ")
Niwetona (Sturminster Newton, Dorset)...............60	"	(960 ")
Boclands (Buckland Newton , Dorset).......................60	"	(960 ")
Sowy (Middlezoy) 120	"	(1920 ")
Hamma (Ham)..50	"	(800 ")
Shapewik' (Shapwick)..60	"	(960 ")
Insula Glastonia (Glastonbury)..............................60	"	(960 ")
Merkedyr' (Marksbury)...40	"	(640 ")
Buddekelege (Butleigh) 65	"	(1040 ")
Streta (Street)..40	"	(640 ")
Waltona (Walton) 72	"	(1152 ")
Escota (Ashcott) 40	"	(640 ")
Pultona (Pilton)...40	"	(2240 ")

TOTAL   1557 perch   (4.7 miles)

4.John of Glastonbury" as translated in "The Chronicles of Glastonbury Abbey" by J.P. Carley notes Abbot Adam of Sodbury's addition to the park.

5.The number of deer in the Park in 1536 is recorded in Valor Ecclesiasticus a copy of which is available in Taunton Library.

6.The small map of the Park is taken from C. Saxton's 1575 map of Somerset re-issued in 1607 with park enclosures clearly marked.

7.Details of E. Rogers appointment are in Cal. Of Letters & Papers of Henry VIII vol. XV page 341.

8.The poaching court case is in The Public Record Office STAC 4/3/66.

9. The 1552 survey is mentioned by Phelps in his "History of Somerset".

10.Letters about the Park in 1555 are to be found in Cal. Of State Papers (Domestic Series) 1601- 03 (addn. 1547-65),p437 item 34.

11.A letter in The Wiltshire Record Office refers to Lord Bruce disparking Pilton Park around 1690. Ref; 1300/324/A.

Section 6

1 information on Thomas Whyting being a tenant at Pilton can be found in ; "The Monastic Grange in Medieval England" by Colin Platt p. 227.

2.The number of Bondmen on Pilton is given in" The Valor Ecclesiasticus"

3.Details of Seymour setting free a villein can be found at S.R.O., DD/AB/26.

4.The letter granting Edward Rogers as keeper at Pilton is contained in the Letters & Papers of Henry VIII, vol. XV, page 341item 733/2, Grants in May 1540

" Edw. Rogers. To be keeper of the chief mansion or house of Pilton ,alias Pulton, Somers., belonging to the late monastery of Glastonbury; and keeper of Pilton Park, with the herbage and pannage of the same park and of Park Hill, and other parcels of land (named)lying within the said park: all which came to the King by the attainder of Richard, the late Abbot: with 2d. a day in each office…"

5.The grant of Edward Seymour's lands including Pilton is given in the Calendar Patent Rolls for 1547-8 and dated on p.118 as 27/7/1547

6.A useful condensed summary of Edward Seymour's life can be found in The Oxford Dictionary of National Biography, including information on Elizabeth's restoration of Edward's lands.

7.Calendar of State Papers 1601-03(addendum for years 1547-65) p. 437 item 34 ,dated 2/4/1555 notes the interest of the Court of Wards in Edwards property at Pilton.

The Wiltshire Record office has many of the records of the Seymour's and particularly relevant is ref:1300/164 dated 1553 listing the lands that Anne wife of the Duke of Somerset was allowed to keep for her son Edward when he was a ward, the list would seem to include Pilton.

8.There are copyholds in S.R.O. DD/AB/33 dated 1646, and 1670: and DD\NL/1 dated 1662 showing the Seymours as Lords of the Manor.

9.There are other relevant documents at The Wiltshire Office, one dated 1695 ref. 1300/277,indicates that Lord Bruce was selling all he could of his wife's estates.

10.Lease to Lady Isabella Bruce can be found at S.R.O. DD/AB/5 1. The Lease is dated 24th. Dec 1690.

11.S.R.O. DD/GL/140 date 1686-1702 lists all Pilton properties in Bruce's possession before the 1719 sale.

12.Further general information on the Gores and Langtons can be found in Robert Dunning's book, " Somerset Families."

13.The conveyance of the Manor to Joseph Langton is to be found at S.R.O. DD/GL/53.

14.Information on the 1996 Lordship sale is available at P.V.H.G. D/103/M.

Section 7

1.Two good general books about the Civil War are "The Civil War in the West", by John Barratt. : and "an Unhappy Civil War", by J. Wroughton. Both have been used in this section.

2.The Oxford Dictionary of National Biography gives details of the Seymour fine.

3.Additional information on the Rebellion can be found in "Wessex Rising " by Douglas Stuckey, and "The Monmouth Rebels" by W. McD Wigfield, which lists all 4,00 names reported to the authorities as supporting Monmouth.

4.The Sedgemoor battlefield was three miles east of Bridgewater in low-lying land between the village of Chetzoy and Westonzoyland.This area is entirely different and some miles away from the Sedgemoor in the western parts of North Wootton.

5.It is mentioned in Preb. Bennett's History (see appendix section15/1 for reference) that bodies from the Rebellion were buried in a field north of the A361 opposite the Old School, and that a stone cannonball was found there.

Section 8

1.Collinson 's History of Somerset p.481 gives references for the pre dissolution Abbots who built up the Manor House, and research by Brian Hale gives Michael of Amesbury as the original builder.

2.S.R.O . T\PH\wat/4 contains the 1315 description of the principal mansion, and more detail given in 1539 by a survey conducted by the court of Augmentation. See also "wealth of Glastonbury Abbey" by Peter Clery.

3.Both Collinson and Phelps in their histories of Somerset indicate that The Manor and its Estate at Pilton was in 1641 in the hands of the Prynne family. However it is likely that this relates only to the Manor House and its accompanying estate, with the Lordship and the other properties remaining with William Seymour(the 2nd. Duke of Somerset).The Prynne acquisition of the Manor House supposedly came about via the marriage of Francis (William Seymour's younger brother) with Frances only daughter of Sir Gilbert Prynne ,Knt. of Allington in Wiltshire. According to Phelps Francis only had a life interest in the Manor House, and when he died it reverted to William.

4.See also section 6 appendix for references to sales of The Manor House and Pilton Lordship.

5.The 1260 dovecote is mentioned in Abbot Fords survey S.R.S. vol.5.

6.Details on the Manors Dovecote are contained in "The Dovecotes of Historical Somerset" by John Mc. Can.

7. Henry Hope had his property surveyed in 1808 before buying and his surveyors report is summarised below The report can be found at S.R.O.ref; DD/FR/25(which also includes Lady Pole's accounts for the house, and rentals from 1829-32.)

'…..........................…..........the house(i.e. The Manor House) is …..…….on a small scale and does not appear ever to have been a mansion of consequence…...…..... the village is very small not more than twenty houses. The inhabitants have the appearance of being healthy and comfortable. Shepton Mallet is the nearest post town….it has a market every Friday abundantly supplied but the prices are beyond that I could have supposed; Mutton, Beef and Veal seven pence a pound, and butter 15d…....…….. ...the estate is well calculated as an investment but as a residence not very desirable in its present state, I examined each inclosure of land very minutely it consists of about 1000 acres of arable and common Pasture and grazing, the whole is in a state of mismanagement most improperly arranged-...£2000 needed to be spent in drainage and irrigation of a large part of the estate as it was too wet...the timber did not appear to be worth near the sum it is fixed at viz. £2500 but I believe no accurate survey has been made. The farm homes are neat & in tolerable repair. The inside of the Mansion is in a very bad state and cannot be made habitable for less than £1000- there is a most magnificent room built at the back of the house 46feet by 24- if the estate is purchased I would recommend its being let in two farms one on each side the stream ….....................… I desired Mr. Lovell one of the trustees for the sale to give me the lowest price, he says £50000- and from what passed I do not believe a less sum will be taken. If the estate does not let on lease for £2000 p.a. a proportionate deduction to be mad e in the price. It therefore is as follows. You will for £50000 have an estate which yielded an immediate interest of 4% with a certainty of a progressive in case of rent,.....................buildings must be worth at least £2000 and timber say one half is what is the computed value £1250--.....................land tax only £30-3-8 for the whole property.'

8. Various deeds for the Pilton Park estate can be found at S.R.O. ref; DD\FR.

9. If Perridge was part of Alhampton its Lordship can be traced in S.R.S. " Feodary of Glastonbury Abbey 1342"Vol. 26., and Feudal Aids vol. IV.

10 .The extracts below are from " The Diary of a West Country Physician" –Diary of Dr. Claver Morris ed. Hobhouse.

21st. March 1710 "………I went to Puridge and ordered that of 33 windows there, 29 should be sufferd to remain". '

21st. January 1721 " Eve Stacy came, and for her husband (he being afraid of the Small Pox) agreed to rent Puridge another year......."

6th. July 1721 " John Middle and his son William Middle went about the grounds with us. I had them to Puridge-House and gave them three bottles of my beer there, which were 9 years old and 8 years in the bottle and yet mantled and was very good and mellow".

10th. November 1722 [extract from his accounts] " [received] Of John Nurse what he sold 2 1/2 lbs. of Elming-Faggots for 15/-; and for Thorning-faggots which he had himself 4/- which I took out in work and 3/- which he is to allow me more in work about staking in the fir-trees" Total=15/-.

26th. March 1723 "After dinner Mr. Lucas and I went in my Calesh to the funeral of Mr. Edward Strode of Ham who was buried at Pilton".

May 16th. 1723 " I finished the putting on the Spurrs and Barrs of my Jack Splatter –dashes (mud leggins). After dinner I went to Puridge to see the masons work on the Stew- Pond, and on the north-end of the Brew – House. I saw my new planted wood at Ring- Well" [NW. Pilton].

June 14th. 1723 "Being this day determined to draw my fish-pond at Puridge I sent early thither a large leg of mutton and 10 penny worth of colliflowers, cabbage and a piece of Ruff'd-beef which was boyld yesterday; a large loaf of bread , a cheese, mustard ,vinegar , salt, butter; a little sauce-pan, two platters, a dozen of Trencher plates, a dozen of knives and forks to them; a table-cloth, three dozen quarts of bottled October beer; twelve quarts of barreled October beer, six nails; sixpenny-nails; and a piece of small card to tye a lead quarter of an hundred weight which I also sent, to the Colander for the Tamkin [plug]Hole. Will Clark yesterday and today carryd in hampiers these things. Molly Mitchell went to dress the mutton,in the morning betwixt 7 and 8 o'clock: at the same time my son, James Keins and my servant George Champion, went also to Puridge.About half an hour past nine, John Johnson my mason (being at work about the Gouts and Brew-House) drew up the Tamkin and the pond ran out in about two hours.........About two we went to dinner. I sent Will Clark home with 12 brace of small carps, to Mr. Slade, for Colonel Brydes at Stoke- Gifford and 3 brace of middling ones to be eaten at home. I put all the rest, being about 190 into the stew-pond and into the house-pond. We came home after 9"

Dr. Claver Morris born 1659, died 1726.Married his 2nd. Wife Elizabeth Jeans [daughter of Edmund Dawe lord of Ditcheat manor & a widow] who brought him property ,she died 1699. He re-married Aug. 1703 to Molly Bragg – bought Perridge for£800 between 1706-1711.He built a house in Wells in 1700/1 and lived in it until his death. His son was born 1709, died 1739. His daughter Betty married a Mr. Burland in 1718 [born 1697],and it was the Burlands who inherited Perridge.

11. Additional information on Perridge House can be found in " The History of Somerset" by Phelps.

12. Preb.. Bennet in his unpublished History of Pilton also traced some of the owners of Perridge. The oldest owner he uncovered was Sir Simon Hewart who passed it to Mr. Heaven who sold it to Squire Pearse in order to buy Lundy Island. It was then sold to Mr. Hayne from Godney and his nephew sold it to Mr. Dobson who sold it to Mr. Edmund Cary from Pylle.

Section 9

1. The complete list of customs can be found in S.R.O. DD\GL/141.

2. Gradually copy holds gave way to leases for three lives, and then leases for 99 years. Copy holds were not formally abolished nationally until the 1922 Property Act It is worth noting here that until the Civil War when Parliament abolished Knight 's fee, all land had been owned by the King and His under lords "held " the land for some form of service or payment. After the abolishment of the fee ,underlords thereafter owned the land freehold , and could do what they liked with it without any future contact with the sovereign.

3. The full details of the enclosure act are at S.R.O. D\P\pilt/20/1/1 together with plans of the areas concerned.

Section 10

1. General books having information on early Christianity in Somerset, include "The Origins of Somerset" by M. Costen, and " Aspects of Somerset History" by T. J. Hunt.

2. Tithe Field Names
Listed below are the Pilton field names from 1838 apportionments[only a few less interesting generic names have been omitted e.g. 7 acre field, /Homefield /north field].Words in (brackets) are to be read as if in front of the field name.

Field name	Approx. acreage
Allas	16
Ash	7
Ashmans Close/Hammers Ash	12
Babyland	5
Back Lane Paddock	2
Backside	10
Bacon Acre	1
Bald Acre	4
Bari Close/Field	6
Barrow Orchard	8
Batch/Batch orchard	10
Batchwood	6
Bathing Pond Plantation	2
Bean Close	12
Becks Paddock	1
Beetle Acre	5
Bendley[Great]	13
Biggs Paddock	3
Blind Orchard	1
Boardens	18
Bonds House Mead	4
Bourns	1
Bower Mead	54
Bowlas(Near)	1
Bottoms	13
Bradleigh/Little Bradley/Hanging Bradley	12
Broke Hedge	7
Breach/Breach orchard	7
Bridge Foot	3
Brimley	17
Bread Close	7
Broad Leaze	16
Brooks Close	20
Browns Close	8
Brush Heath/Hanging Brush Heath	25
Burbages	8
Bullocks Path	22
Burford Cross/Burford Ground/Mead	13
Burrells Gate	3
Bushing	24
Butchers Arms Inn	0
Butty Clos	9
Butts	2
Carps	11
Carters Bridge Ground	7
Cattles	16
Chaise(middle)	12
Chanters /Chanters Barn/Ham	18
Cookford(part)	2
Chapmans Mead/ Bach	13
Charlton(in)	1
Chaseys Close	7
Chizel	4
Clapper	3
Cliffs(the)	3
Closing Field	5
Cleeve	8
Clover Ground	6
Cole Close	4
Combe/ North Combe	55
Compton Field	2
Compton Lane/ Compton Wood	20
Common field	5
Cornfield Wall	11
Cottles Paddock	8
Crab Tree Close	4
Crooked Close	14
Crown(old) Gardens	1
Culverwell	8
Cummel	5
Cutlers close	8
Dicks Orchard	2
Doulton Mead	1
Dowel/s/Turkey Dowel	63
Drang	2
Draugt Acre	2
Draw Meadow	7
Dry close	12
Dunkertons Ground	4
Dyes house	18
Easley	31
East Hill	23
Elliots Hole	3
Elvy	4
Fair (the) ground	3
Flatwood	2
Folly	4
Fossway	3
Foxhole	52
Fench Grass Land	5
Frogwell	10
Friass Oven	5
Friezeland	1

Furnell (nut)	11	Long Bank Orchard	1
Furze Close	2	Long Close/Long Croft	5
Ganwell	32	Longlands/Longlands Orchard/close	24
Garston (Kings)	6	Longleys	9
Gear	3	Long Mead Orchard	4
Gorewell	15	Luggs	5
Gose Meafow	8	Maggs	8
Greatleys	4	Marl Ground	5
Green Ledge	51	Mere (High)	4
Guard Acre	4	Merrys Ground	6
Gully Land	17	Meet (Part) Furnell	3
Guzzle Brook	4	Mill Paddock/Mill Meadow	3
Ham Lane/Paddock/Green/Long-	35	Mitchell Mead/Orchard	4
Ham Wood	72	Much Leaze/Muck Leaze	15
Harbour(Cold)	33	Neat/Neat Paddock	3
Harps	3	Nursery	7
Hartley	25	Nut Hedge	7
Hatches Paddock	1	Oat Hill	20
Hatchings	6	Oatley	22
Hawkwell	11	Oldley	2
Hayes(Silver)/Middle Hayes/Hoop Hayes	14	Oxleaze	18
Henleys Thorn	9	Pagets (Late)	3
Highcroft	3	Paines Meadow	31
Hills/Old/Great/Hill Paddock	62	Parfits(Little)	4
Hinney Mead	13	Park Hill Ground	8
Hinton	23	Park (High)	16
Hitching Hill	12	Peak (The)	2
Hitchings/Lower/Middle/Top	26	Pease Close	18
Holts	37	Piece	14
Holt Pier	5	Perridge/Perridge House/Hill/Orchard	21
Hunwell	27	Pidlands	13
Hounds Cock Rice	3	Pilton Field	17
Huntling	5	Pilton Wood	17
Hurds Orchard/Hurds Close	2	Pict Under Wood	1
Hurn	6	Platerwell/Adjoining Platerwell Lane	8
Husk	15	Pond Ground	24
Ivy Mead	16	Pondhay	8
Kennel Ground	3	Poor Ground	5
Kidney Mead	3	Postmans Acre	2
Kinney Mead	5	Prospect	27
Kite Oak	3	Pursefurlong	8
Knowle/knowles	37	Pylle Lane	9
Knowle (part) hill/Past Knowle Hll	24	Quar	21
Knowle(in) Lane/Ridgeway Knowle Ground	5	Redlake (Adjoining)	2
Ladden(Hill)	6	Redland	1
Lane End/Lane Gate	5	Rickbarton Close	6
Lamberts Close	12	Ridgeway	44
Lamberts Hill	35	Ridgeway on Knowle Ground	3
Latts Hill	15	Ridgeway Cleeves	7
Laverly	12	Riding	9
Layers five acres	5	Rife	14
Legs	4	Ringwell	10
Leys/Leigh/New Leaze	30	Round Mead	7
Lichall	42	Rowmead	12
Lights	12	Rush	9
Link(s) Meadow	27	Sarch/Past Sarch	20
Lobthorn	6	Sawpit Paddock	2
Lodge Paddock	2	Scammells (by) Barn	1
Long back Orchard	3	Scones Ground	4

Shambles	9	Tynings (new)	5
Shay	16	Toll House & Garden	1
Shepton (Part) Field	3	Townsend	12
Shordle	25	Tully Close	2
Sideland	40	Tutty Close	8
Siggrly	2	Turnpike Ground/Turnpike Paddock	11
Slades Orchard	1	Twine Woods	6
Sleight/Great Sleights	29	Warbutts Batch	2
Show (Great)	8	Warfords Batch	2
Society (in) Ground/(above)/New Society Gd.	6	Warrens	5
Splots	3	Watkins (late(	7
Stakeways/Past Stakeways	8	Watts Orchard	1
Stall Ground	18	Webbs Ash/ Webbs Orchard	16
Stalway	2	Well Close/ (past)	10
Stallwell	15	Wellsway (in) common Field	3
Standgrove	17	Well Ground	7
Starwell Acre	1	Wellings	2
Starre Acre	5	Westholme	28
Stocks Orchard	4	Westleys Wood	22
Stock (Happen)	5	West Hill	34
Stokes/ Stokes Stye	1	Whitecroft	12
Stone field/Stone Ground/orchard	46	Whitegate	18
Strafe	1	Whitelake	16
Strap	6	Whitestone	18
Strodes Mill	1	Winterlane	1
Studley	28	Wining Lake Ground	9
Stump Cross (near)	3	Wood Ground/ Wood Mead	31
Sugs	13	Woods (short)	3
Summer Leaze	26	Wootton Field	28
Sutleigh	7	Worthy	11
Tidcomb	3	Young Orchard	1
Tinings	28		

The source for the above names is S.R.O. ref; DD\CC\B\325174; the original tithe map is also available at the S.R.O. ref; D\P\pilt\3\2\3 a tracing of which is available in the history groups archives.

3. .The information on Hamwood's fine is from Preb. Bennets unpublished history. S.R.O. D\P\pilt\23\18.

4. Details on the church building have been mainly taken from an article by Rev. T. Holmes published in , S.A.N.H.S. 1888,and a copy available in P.V.H.G. D/050/2.

5. More details on the church and its legend is to be found in " Stories and Events " from Pilton Church published in the church's own guide to St. John the Baptist.

6. Michael Costen gave a series of lectures on Pilton, which are summarised in P.V.H.G. D/016.

7.An attempt to trace back the Joseph legend has met with little success. The two early historians most frequently quoted about Somerset (Phelps 1839 and The Reverend John Collinson 1796) spent some time discussing aspects of Pilton Church but made no mention of the legend. The Somerset Archaeological & Natural History Society published two articles on The Church before 1899 and on neither occasion was the Legend mentioned. Other interested parties have commented on the church in the 19th. Century ,including an extensive article in a local paper. Any such legend would almost certainly have been mentioned if it was known about, but no, not a word.. The first mentions of it that could be found were claims made by Preb. Bennett (The vicar at Pilton 1899-1934) early in the 20th. Century .He also wrote a play about the legend. His support for the idea seemed to be based mainly on the information that Joseph was known to be a merchant, and that it was also known that lead and other precious metals from the Priddy area and Charterhouse were traded with the Romans. He also believed that Pilton was a port in Roman times. It is not clear why anyone would choose to get to either Priddy or Charterhouse via Pilton when coming from The Severn Channel even if Pilton was a port or harbour in those times. However according to Michael Costen of Bristol University, the work of geologists and archaeologists show conclusively that the sea never extended permanently as far as Pilton in Roman times. Part of the difficulty about this issue is that at one time it was thought that the *Pyl-* in Pilton derived from an old Welsh word meaning creek or harbour, and indeed Pilton was frequently spelt " Pulton", interpreted as meaning "Pooltown". This interpretation is no longer believed by those who have studied place name origins (see section 2).

8.. Research into the Non Conformists was conducted by the late David Chapman, and additional information is taken from the "Rise of Methodism,Preaching of the Wesleys and of Whitefield" by William E.H. Lecky.

9.A 1902 Trust Deed for the Ebenezer Chapel gives information on the building .S.R.O . ref. D\N\mca/4/3.

10.. It is also worth noting that Preb. Bennet in his history mentions that a fourth church(or Mission House) once existed in Pilton. This was at Cannards Grave, and existed from around the late 19th. to the early years of the 20th. Century. Little information has been found about it other than it was started by Miss Trevelyan and built on land donated by Mr John Hoskins.

Section 11

1. S.R.S. vol. 4 "Pre-Reformation churchwardens accounts" covers some of Pilton's churchwardens accounts between 1498 and 1530. The short extracts included in the text are from this source, but much more detail is available in the full accounts.

2. The churchwardens accounts for the years 1625-1641 can be found in S.R.O. D\P\pilt/4/1/3.The extract below is the complete accounts for the 12 months from April 1626 to March 1627, an well illustrate the range of activities which the churchwardens became involved with.

" The 28th. Daye of March Anno D'mi 1627 ....

The accompts of Michael Scott and Thomas Hall Churchwardens for the yeare past A.D. 1626 now ended was taken and ve(tted? .before Mr Nathaniel Abbott Vicar of Pilton & the Parishioners there the day & year above said. Their disbursements as followeth

Pd. unto William Lane Constable for the Maymed souldiers & hospitals against Ilchester sessions	8s. 8 d.
Item paid for glasinge the Church windows.	14 d
Item paid for a bottle for the parish use to fetch wine in for the Communions	2s .4d.
For Common fyne for the Churchowse	1d.
pd. For 6 quarts of wine for the Communion against Whitsuntide	6s. 0d.
For bread then	2d
Item given unto two briefs laid out by Mr. Abbott afore the 16 of Julie	12 d.
Given a poor traveylor with a pass	2 d
pd.unto John Rogers the one halfe of the Widdow Slades -12d. Which he could not rec.....	6 d.
Item for the parish dykeinge done by John Rossiter this yeare. Pd.	2 d
Item given to a poore traveylor about Michelmas	3 d.
Item to another poore man another tyme	2 d.
For the two service booked for Wensdaies	2s 0 d
Pd.the Dutches Bayliff the churchowse rent this year	1 d
Item paid the Constable for the Maymed Souldiers & hospitals for Midsomer quarter	8s. 8 d
Item pd. The Constable Michaells Quarter	8s. 8 d
Pd. for 7quarts of wine for the Communions .....All saints day & the Sunday after	7s. 0 d
For bread for those Communions	2 d pd.
Charges at Visitation this yeare for the Ordinary & Register Churchwardens & 2 men & dinner	10s ?
Item for exhibitinge the bill of presentment	20...?
Item given a poore traveylinge souldier	2 d
Item to another poore man comming out of Turkey	2 d.
Item paid John Stagg for makinge walls against the Marie Hay being the parish fence	8s. ?
Item for 15 loads of stones digged for that worke at 2d. At each loade with filling the Pitt	3s 1 d
For carriage of those 15 loads at 3d. A load	4s 9 d
Given two traveylinge souldiers of the Low Cuntries	2 d
To another souldier with a pass given	2 d
Item pd. For 10 quarts & a pint of wine for the Communions at Christmas	10s .6 d
And for bread then	2 d
Given to a brief to one John Walker for £800 loss at sea by we......... in this Countie	6 d.
Pd. For two new bell ropes for the tenor & second bell	6s. 4 d
Pd. Mr. Abbott for the last praye book sett for th? By the K?inge of Denmarke	4 d
Pd. Mr. Abbott wich he laid out for a briefe	6 d
Item given to a brief for a church in Dorsettshire	7 d.
Item given to a poor man coming out of captivty out of the low Cuntries	2 d

Item laid out to another brief for loss at sea delivered in the presence of Mr. Abbott	12 d.
To a souldier commmin out of Argyer?	2 d
For a load of good .....stones & the drawinges	6d.
Paid John Masters for hedgeing the north side of the Marie hay	6d.
For 200 & half of plants & the setting	14?
Pd. For a plante to Thomas Headland to lay upon the bench on east side the Chancell door	2s.5d?
Paid William Hurman for castinge 82 lbs. of old lead after? The rateof 4s. The 100	2s 10?
Pd. him for 57 lbs. of new lead at 1 1/2d.the lb.	7s. 1d
Pd. Him for 8 lb. Of sowder at 10d. The lb.	6s. 8d
For a day & half & work to him & his sonne on the top of the tower	3s.
For woode to make fire to heate the plumbers tooles	12d ?
Paid John Ridewood for tymber,nailes&worke in tymbering under the lead of the tower	illeg.
Pd. W. Dunkerton for a planck to lay on the bench on west of ye Chancell door & for a Broad stone laid at the Chancell doore to John Ridewood & work about the plants & seates &mending the church hatches	illeg.
Pd. for 18 quarts of wine for Communions Palm Sunday Sheare thursday EasterEave &Easter day.....	18s..?
For bread for these communions	9d.
Pd. For washing the Surplesses severall tymes & the ther/n lynnnen once this year	illeg.
For parchment to copie the register booke into the office at Wells	illeg
John Poole for 5 daies work & halfe about the churchowse wall & at the benches at the Channcell door	5s...?
To John Powell for 3 parts of a daie woorke	8d?
Pd. .... Bartlett for attendinge poore	18?
Item for 9 loades of stones drawect for the said Worke	2s..?
Item for carriage of these 9 loades of stones	3s 3d
. Item for two loades of morter	6d.
Item for two sackes of lyme	16d
Pd. To John Wilmott for attending the mason at the churchhaie wall	4d
For cariage of the stone at Chancell Door from John Ridwoode	3 d
For carriage of one of the planks out of Highwood.	3d
To Thomas paine for his frewor?? about the the t?ower glasses a plate of fet? For one of the planks mending two of the church latches with a catch and nailes }	2s10d
Pd. The Clarke his yeares stipend for plaing the organs Wrighting the register book & wrighting forus & Casting the accompts	20s
Pd.John Pooke to finish the worke at the Mariie Haie Wall	3s.
. m totall of all their disbursments is	£ 9 – 16s -6 1/2d.
Memorandum. John Ridewood is unpayed of six wages for ringing Curfue,keeping the clock& the bells	18s..?
Item John Copp his yeares stipend for keeping out doggs & blowing the organs	6s 8d.
The charge or receits of the said wardens in the year	
Inprimis they are charged as recd. Of the old wardens at the entrance into office with the some of.....	illeg.
Item they are charged with the booke of rates of the parisheioners their yeare the some of	£8-lleg
ecd.The yearely Annuitye from the wardens of Wootten as ... from their Chappell to the Church p.a	5s.
tem recd. The rent of the parishe land this yeare	3s. 4d.
Item recd.The gifte ofMr Richard Wattes by his will gave church	12d
Recd .for rent of 2 dozen of Church vessels to Walter Withers	4d.
. Sum totall of the receits is	£9 -11s. – 3d

So the receits is lesse than the disbursments by 5s.-3 1/2d & is due to Mr. Scott from the new Church wardens chosen for the yeare following 1627 viz. William Middle & Hugh Warford. Memorundum that the 5s.-3 1/2d. With the 18s. Due to John Ridewood & 6s.-8d. Due to John Copp amounts to in the whole due to the former wardens   29s. 11 1/2d "

{n.d some words/payments were illegible in the original manuscript and are either denoted' illeg' or if partially il legible ,denoted with a '?' }

3. An account of the system of briefs is included in" The Parish Chest" by W.E.Tate

4. Reference to playing games in the churchyard are to be found in S.R.O. D\P\pilt/4/1/5

Section 12

1. Background information on early road legislation can be found in Tates'The Parish Chest.

2. See S.R.O. DD\DK/15-16 for the original Table of Tolls.

3. TheVestry Minute Book 1831-1858 can be found at S.R.O.D/P/pilt/9/1/1.

4. Below are some of the Vestry proceedings arising from the 1831 £100 fine.

January 8th.1832   The inhabitants of Pilton are requested to meet in the Vestry Room of this Church on Thursday next at 10 o clock in the morning to take into consideration an order for defraying the expenses of the indictment against a certain road or way at Redlake in the Parish of Pilton.

Thomas Phelps (Waywarden of Westholme & Holt)

January 12th. 1832   At a Vestry held this day pursuant to the above notice it was ordered that one hundred pounds be borrowed to pay the fine passed by the justices at the last sessions against the Parish of Pilton, and we whose names are hereunto subscribed (on behalf of the Parish of Pilton) do hereby undertake to become responsible to Mr. Townsend who has offerd to lend the said one hundred pounds for the repayment of the same with lawful Interest for the same,

Robt. Orledge   Cha.. Orledge (Churchwarden)   Francis Hamwood   Thos. Reeves
Mathew Tuk   Thos. Phelps   John Gough   S. Allen   Mr. Hawkins   .   John Stokes
William Gould   Wm. Orledge   James Corpe   Wm. Broad.

At the same Vestry it was further resolved that a Councils   opinion be taken if necessary whether the said road is to be repaired at the expense of the parish at large or the Tithing of Westholme & Holt

March 29th.   At a Vestry meeting held this day pursuant to advertisement dated March the 22nd. Instant for receiving tenders for making the whole road that is indicted at Redlake, finding Stones and Hauling the same to the satisfaction of the viewing Magistrate. I the undersigned do hereby agree to do the said work to the satisfaction of the said Magistrates and to complete the same one full week before the next Midsummer Quarter Sessions at or for the sum of thirty six pounds, the parish giving the stones already quarrid in Mr. Pearces field by Mr. Clerk, and paying the damage in the centre of such Quarring to Mr. Pearce.

The stones to be 9 inches deep in the centre of the road , seven inches at the side, and the road twelve feet wide

(signed)   James Green

April 24th. 1832   At a vestry held this day it is ordered that a rate of six pence in the pound be made and collected for making the Road and paying the expenses of the Indictment against the Road at Redlake

Clerk Curate ; James Bethell & Charles Orledge (churchwardens); Robt. Townsend; C. Moody; Mathew Teek

May 3rd. 1832   At a vestry held this day pursuant to notice given on Sunday last , during Divine Service. It is ordered that each Tithing shall pay as follows towards paying the Expenses of the Indictment and making the Road at Redlake (viz) Pilton Tithing £28-17s.-81/2d., East Compton £16=5=0, West Compton £13=17=81/2, Westholm & Holt with Wootton £33=9=9 & Ham £13=6=6. And in case any person or persons refusing to pay his or their share or proportion of the assessment made on him or them it is ordered that Messers Phipps and Hyatt do proceed against him or them for its recovery according to law.

Thos. Phelps   James Bethell   Is. Gould   Wm. Orledge   Jos Green   C. Moody
Wm. Broad   Wm. Gould   Robt. Orledge   John Gough   Richard Jeffery   Alan Hiscox.

5. Information on the details of the local Turnpike Trusts has been based mainly on J.B.Bentley's " Somerset Roads: the legacy of the Turnpikes phase 2." 1987.

6. The main source of information on the stage coaches is taken from ' The Coaching Era' by G. Body & R. Gallop.

7. Helpful information on local trains is available in " Lost Railways of Somerset " by S. York; and "Somerset In The Age Of Steam " P. Stanier.

Section 13

1 Information on the schools in Somerset is contained in " The Millennium Book", produced by the Somerset Archaeological & Natural History Society.

2. Information on the number of pupils -1890 is from P.V.H.G. D/015/p .

3.Original Board of Education Reports for 1902/3/4 are in S.R.O. C/E/4/380/318, and some details of school activities after the second World War are in P.V.G.H. D/237.

4.Summarised below are some of the school memories of Muriel E. Beale (1889-1980) a descendant of John Beale who lived her school life in Pilton. The memories were kindly provided by C.S.B Smith , her son, and cover the years 1892-1903 (P.V.H.G.L/005).

"……………..............………..As I went to school at the age of three, I soon learned to read …………Ten minutes playtime morning and afternoon even for three years old was all we had. Sometimes on sunny mornings the headmaster would relent and we would get an extra ten minutes, giving us a little more time in the field opposite to play or make daisy chains…………In playtime on Fridays we would watch the animals being driven to market three miles away. They had perhaps come some distance and on very hot days the sheep especially looked very distressed. The pigs always got a ride ,they were too wise to move fast………………As the school was a National Church of England one, the longest lesson of the day was devoted to Scripture. We learnt the Commandments, the Duties, The Catechism, the Sacrament of the Lords Supper, Parables, Miracles off by heart..The three year olds learnt texts, **A- A** soft answer turneth away wrath , **B-B** elieve in the Lord Jesus Christ and thou shalt be saved. **C-C** ome unto me all ye that labour….and so on through the alphabet. With what gusto we repeated Jesus wept, and Quench not the spirit, because these two were the shortest. We learnt the colours;

> This ball is blue, and a lovely colour too.
> This ball is yellow, what a pretty fellow.
> This ball is green, as is plain to be seen.

Large sheets of thick paper about fifty four inches by thirty six inches, joined together at the top were hung upon the wall. For the lesson it was taken down and supported on an easel. On the first sheet was the alphabet in small letters and capitals; which learned first. Then on the next sheet showed the joining up of letters; cab, dab, cat, rat, and so on. Children soon learnt to read……..There were pictures of animals on the walls, both wild and tame…………When I went to school first , I had to take two pence every Monday morning, but this was stopped soon afterwards.

The infants all sat in two galleries, one had a bench at the bottom for the newcomers, the three year olds to sit on. One gallery was for the youngest classes, the three years old, the fours and the dull fives. The other was for the bright fives, the sixes and the dull sevens. There were two teachers both Article 68's earning about forty pounds a year. One was a stranger to the village so must have been lodged, fed and clothed on that sum. In the big school, divided from the infants by a partition, was the headmaster who taught standard four, five and six and another article 68 who taught the lower standards, All subjects were taken together except arithmetic which had to be taken separately for each standard. ……………Time was spent on plaiting coloured papers, stringing beads, learning to count on the abacus, writing pothooks and hangers on slates, singing and reciting. We all had to work very hard, for upon our labours grants of money from the government for the school depended. Inspectors….brought strange books from which we read, set us sums and generally examine us. If we passed at the age of six we went into the big school.

There were no organised games such as football or cricket. In the playground we played round games such as, I sent a letter to my love, Fill the gap. Stag, Ring of Roses,Cock Robin is dead and lies in his grave, a long singing and acting game.

> Oh here's a pretty little girl of mine'
> She brought me a bottle of wine.

Nuts in May, and 'are you ready for the fight, we are the Romans'……A very charming game went thus;

> Last night when we parted
> I left you broken hearted
> Upon the green mountain, there stands your young man,
> Choose your lover, choose your lover
> Choose your lover, farewell.
> In the ring love, In the ring love,
> In the ring love, farewell.

The girls skipped, and the boys played marbles,conkers in the autumn, and spun tops, also boys and girls had hoops. The girls wooden ones and the boys iron which they bowled with an iron rod. By the time we left Infants School at age six or seven, we knew all the multiplication tables up to twelve times, could read and write, add, subtract and multiply, and divide with numbers, could say the Lord's Prayer, the Apostles Creed, the first four commandments, and many recitations, songs and hymns.

In the big school we worked harder than ever. All the new tables had to be learned, money, measures of capacity,weight,area and length. We began to learn geography. The geographical features round the coasts of the British Isles, mountains, bays, headlands, hills and rivers off by heart. We had a perfect picture in our minds and could almost draw a map blindfold. But most important of all we began to learn grammar, beginning in standard one with the parts of speech,proper,common and abstract nouns, the comparison of adjectives, genders, cases, moods.tenses,numbers and everything leading up to the parsing of words and the analysing of sentences. ....Lord Ullins Daughter, The Wreck of Hesperus, We are Seven, were typical recitations for the lower classes. The Ancient Mariner, The Deserted Village, Edinburgh after Flodden , for the higher classes. The poems were printed on large cards which were given out before the lesson, collected about halfway through, and we were then head on the amount we had been given to learn.

There was no physical education. Once a week we went into the playground and did military exercises, forming fours, standing at ease, turning to the right and to the left, and marching. If wet, exercise took place in the school with dumb bells as we sang ,sending our arms up and down in and out to the rhythm.

Four and one ,two three four

One two three four

One two three four, and

One two three four.

Arithmetic was a very serious subject, and a great deal of time was spent on it, so that at twelve years of age ,we were dong compound interest, profit and loss, stocks and shares, decimals and recurring decimals..During the afternoons, the girls spent their time on needlework, while the boys were taught drawing. Socks and stockings were knitted. These were sold to the villagers for one shilling a pair. Pillow cases were made by the younger children and these were sold for four pence each. The elder girls made print dresses, chemises and other garments for themselves. Some afternoons were spent in making samples of gathering and stroking, patching and darning, herring-boning and feather stitching. The school staff consisted of one college certificated headmaster, and three untrained uncertificated assistants, two in the infants' department, and one to help the headmaster with the older children. These three went under the name of Article 68's.Their salaries must have been very small , perhaps about thirty or forty pounds a year.

The headmaster received ninety pounds a year, and his house and coal. He was short, with a red face and bright blue eyes. He was strict but not cruel. He was a cultured man, but rather inactive, and he did not cultivate his small vegetable garden. He was fond of dogs and bred black Aberdeen terriers.. The church Choir was trained by him,, and he played the organ for no payment whatever. He had a nice light tenor voice with which he entertained us, singing comic duets with his wife at the school concert which took place every year. In the big school there was a harmonium, on which the headmaster played the accompaniment to many delightful songs.. He had five children, all very handsome, his wife was a very pretty woman, but rather proud….........He received his training at Exeter Collage for teachers, ,….and as she was one of the Article 68's teaching in the infants' school she led a very busy life. They had a good charwoman who also cleaned the school and was paid a shilling a day.

In school we wrote with pencils on slates. The small children had little slates, and they were gradually increased in size as the children got older. They were collected at the end of each writing or arithmetic lesson and the large ones in bulk were very heavy. A small piece of rag or sponge was taken to school every day, and used slates were spat on and wiped clean. Once a week, copy books were handed out and we learnt to writ e with ink, capital letters, small letters, and then joining up, in a very nice round hand, which I still use today;..........

Every year a school concert was organised. Actions, songs, recitations, duets, dialogues were given by the children. The room was generally packed, as entertainments were very few and far between. Sometimes the best performances were asked to go and perform in other villages. We were packed into wagons and were driven slowly along the dark country lanes which seemed very mysterious at night. Sometimes at morning school we were told to bring a penny in the afternoon as there was to be a travelling show. Perhaps it would be a Punch and Judy show (or songs and conjuring tricks). We finished at half past three on those days………Children from a distance of two or three miles brought their mid-day meal, but those with only a mile to go generally went home…….children often got very w et in rainy weather and coats were put round the stove, where they steamed away all morning, but they sat in their wet boots as wellingtons for children had not been invented.

The day before inspections we were told …..,and on the morning the girl's put on clean pinafores, every girl wore one, and the boys put on clean collars, rather narrow starched little collars(Eton).Face and hands had to be extra clean, and hair well-brushed. Most girls had long hair. A small piece was taken from each side, pulled back and tied at the top giving a plain appearance to the face. One or two girls had fringes, but their hair was always long and left hanging, no plaits were worn. Both inspections lasted all day…….The Diocesan Inspector was a tall dark charming man. The small children loved him, after putting the elder ones to work, writing from memory parables, miracles, lives of prophets, each child with a different theme. He came into the infants room and we were asked questions about Daniel, Moses, Noah, David and other well known people of the bible. We repeated the catechism,...............I was very happy at school and when I got home at night in winter, I would sometimes arrange all the cushions on the sofa and taught them. Before we went home at twelve o'clock we sang Grace-

Be present at our table Lord
Be here and everywhere adored
These creatures bless and grant that we
May feast in Paradise with thee

And when we returned at two o'clock we sang

We thank you Lord for this our food
But more because of Jesus' Blood
May manna to our souls be given
The bread of life sent down from heaven

There were 120 children in the school which was divided in two by a partition, half woodland the top half glasss.All the older children were in the larger part, about 70 of them, the rest in the other which had galleries instead of desks, which the older children used. These had no lockers, but there were long benches to sit on, so everything had to be given out..........This meant a lot of cupboard space and they lined the walls . A bench was placed at the bottom of the gallery for the new three year olds, it was necessary for the gallery for the smallest was always full. When I had my seat there , I was once late for school, my sister and brother had gone without mesas I went up the side door which was used for infants, the headmaster happened to look out of the window of the upper school. Seeing me he made a gesture as if to say " hurry up". This upset me so much that I wept all morning until playtime. ......away from school many of them spoke in the dialect of the country, using such expressions as ' cassent' for can't you, 'bissent' for are you, 'oot' for will you, and 'art' are you.......speech was never so broad in the district as it was in the south west.

The Schoolrooms were heated by stoves burning coal, one in the infants room, and two in the bigger room. It always seemed quite cosy.......There were no facilities for washing or attending to cuts and bruises, if an accident occurred the patient was taken into the schoolmaster's house and the wound dressed in the kitchen, and as the playground was not asphalted, gravel rash was fairly frequent. There was a water tap outside in the road with an iron mug attached to the pipe on a chain, so if thirsty one could get a drink of water. The lavatories for the boys separated from the girls by a high wall, were quite good for the period. At the back of the seat there was a small box which contained peat. The box had a handle which when pulled scattered the peat over the contents in the pan. These pans were emptied on a pile behind a large shed where we played in wet weather once a week, and the pile stayed there for about a month when a man came round with a horse and wagon and it was taken away. There was no smell.......

We had 8 weeks holiday in the year, a fortnight at Christmas, a week at Easter, the same at Whitsuntide, and a month in the summer. There were no half term holidays, no sports day or games...., but we had one extra day for the Sunday School treat if it did not take place in the holiday, and we also had a day's holiday to celebrate the Diamond Jubilee of Queen Victoa........the only relaxation I remember was for the three or four year old children. On very hot days if we seemed a little sleepy, we were allowed to put our heads on our folded arms and have a nap. Also on fine days we went into the dusty playground and played round games such as

Ring a Ring of roses
A pocket full of posies
Atishoo Atishoo
We all fall down

The cows are in the meadow
Lying fast asleep
Atishoo Atishoo
We all get up again

Discipline was kept not only at school, but in the village, and any complaint brought punishment in its wake. Four or five boys were sometimes lined up for the cane, after some farmer had complained that his cattle or sheep had been chased, or his apples stolen."

Section 14

1. Below is one month's payments to the poor ,taken from S.R.O.D\P\pilt/4/1/7 Overseers Accounts 1836-61

Pd. to the poor 5 wks.   April1835

		£	s.	d.
Andrews	Anne		14-6	
Andrews	George		12- 6	
Beard	George		15- 0	
Biggs	George		17- 6	
Boyer	Eliz.		6- 0	
Broderips--family		1	0- 0	
Broderip	William		15- 0	
Carpenter	James	1	2- 6	
Chetman	Ann		5- 6	
Coles	Harvey		2- 0	
Collins	james	1	10- 0	
Collins	Hannah		6- 0	
Cox	Ambrose		15-0	
Cox Widow	Widow		12-0	
Dix	Richard		12- 6	
Dunkerton	Family		8- 6	
Dyke	Eliza		7- 6	
Dyke	Thomas		15- 0	
Fear	Mary		10- 0	
Forehead	John		12- 6	
Fry	Daniel	1-`	0- 0	
Fry	Widow		10-0	
Gane	George		8- 6	
Griffen	Robert		12- 0	
Grove	Sarah		8- 6	
Hankman	William	1	12- 0	
Heard	James		10- 0	
Hill	Abraham	1	2- 6	
Hill	Edith		10- 0	
Hill	Hannah		7- 6	
Hoares--child			2- 6	
Humphries	Ann		6- 0	
Hurly	Ann		7- 6	
Hyman	Susanna		5- 0	
Jacobs	Ann		10- 0	
Lambert	Samuel		15- 0	
Lewis	Ann		3-0	
Lewis	James		10 0	
Masters	James		12-6	
Milborne	James		12- 6	
Morgan	Eliz.		15- 6	
Morgan	Robert		5- 0	
Nurse	Sarah		17- 6	
Nurse	Widow	1	5- 6	
Oats?	Sarah		6- 0	
Pike	Renben	1 -	2- 6	
Pike	Robert		19- 0	
Sage	Ann		10-0	
Sage	Job		15-0	
Sims	David	1	0- 0	
Somers	Widow		6-0	
Speed	Thomas		12- 6	
Stevens	Jane		7- 6	
Stride	Betsy		10- 0	
Tippetts	Rose		10-0	
Vining	Sarah		10- 0	
Vinings	child/ren		19- 0	

		£	s.	d.
Watts	Widow		10- 0	
Wilcox	Mary		19- 0	
Williams	James		12-6	
Woolley	James `		10 -0	
Given in distress				
Bellinger	Samuel		3- 6	
Beal	Widow		1- 0	
Beard	George		2- 0	
Bishop	John		3- 0	
Broderip	William		1- 0	
Broderps boy [jacket & shrt]			4- 5	
Broderips lodging			6- 0	
Cleeves	James		1- 0	
Carpenter	James		1- 0	
Collins	James jun.		7- 6	
Collins	Hannah		- 6	
Cook	George		2- 6	
Cook	Thomas		6- 0	
Cook	Mary,Ann		3- 6	
Cooks boy[smock & frock]			5- 0	
Hurley John & wife			11- 6	
Hurley	William		8- 0	
Jacobs	John	2	5- 0	
Lambert[doctor for]			5- 0	
Lane	William		10- 0	
Letters			3-11	
Lewis	William		13- 6	
Midland	George		1- 0	
Martin	William	1	4- 3	
Martins maid for washing			-3	
Millards	wife	1	0	0
Naidment	James		6- 0	
Nurse	John		1- 0	
Pike	Robert	1	4- 0	
Pke	Renbes wife		- 6	
Sge	Ann		- 6	
Stacey	Samuel		5- 6	
Stephens	Jane		1- 0	
Stone	John		6- 0	
Strode[Isaac, for Leicester]		6 - 7	- 0	
Strode	Jane	1	4-6	
Townsend	Hester		5- 0	
Watch	George		10- 0	
Williams	James		0- 6	
Webbs	son		1- 0	
Webb	Stephen		5- 0	
Atending justices meeting			2- 6	
inquest on Sarah Strode			18- 0	
journey to wells			2- 6	
signing rate and expenses			4- 6	
Lodging for nurse Cleeves			6- 0	

April total =£58- 18s-7d.

2. A detailed account of Poor Law legislation is contained in W.E.Tate's " The Parish Chest.

3. Vestry Minutes for 1831-58 are to be found at S.R.O. D\P\pilt/9/1/1

4.Details of a month's occasional payments to the poor are summarised below

Dec 15th. 1831   At a Vestry held this day it is agreed to allow the poor as follows

William Lambert a coat   .James Williams a pair of shoes .   James Carpenter some hessian for a bed tie. Sarah Vinnnig 6d.per week advanced & a petticoat.   Mac Chesney a shift.   Patience Bryant a petticoat. Ann Jacob a shift.   Geo Lamberts oldest boy pr. Of trowsers.   Widow Somers pay to be advanced 6d. per week.   Sam' Bellenger pr. of shoes.   Rose James a blanket.   Sam' Stacey Junior a blanket t   George Beard to allowed a shilling a week.   Sam' Lambert pr. of shoes. Job Sage a Shirt. Stephen Woolley pr. of shoes. Betty Griffen a blanket. Thomas Biggs 8 yds. of Callico. James Naidment some hessian for a bed tie. Richard Dix a blanket. James Fry shirt & shift.. David Fry a blanket.   James Fear a shirt.   James Williams 6d. pay. Sally Thomas pair of shoes .Stevens boy some clothes. John Torchead a blanket.   James Cleeves a jacket & shirt .John Stride 2 blankets and some Hessian for a bed .Thomas Laver pr. of shoes. John Cox 6 yds. 0f Callico .James Lewis 6 yds. of Callico. George Lewis pr. of shoes. Hannah Collins 6d. a week more. Abrm. Hill a shirt. James Pike 5d. in distress. James Collins Junior a shirt. John Millard 2s.6d. a week. Reuben Pike a shirt. Speeds wife a Gown .Widow Cox a blanket. Wm. Lane a blanket. Some bedding etc. for Hoares children. 2 blankets. William Dyke a blanket . 2Blankets for the poor House.   Elizabeth Sims is to be paid 4d. per week for washing for the poor people in the poor House, Keeping the House clean and doing what is generally wanted to be done in the house. Mary Wilcox a blanket. A coffin for Millards child. Thos. Cook a Blanket.

5. May 5th. 1846 at a vestry meeting held this day It was resolved that George Turner be apprehended and brought to justice to be dealt with according to Law for leaving his wife and family chargeable to this Parish, the expenses attending the same to be paid out the Poor Rate.

6. Removal orders information is obtainable at S.R.O. Q/SR/312/161 & Q/SR/310//10.

7.Some information on Workhouses was obtained from www.workhouses.org.uk

8. A copy of the Sun murder report is available in P.V.H.G. D/242.

Section 15

1 The Pilton Village History Group's 1988 publication, " A Walk Through Pilton's Past", has been unavailable for a number of years. It was written and researched by the late Brian Hale who visited and surveyed the individual houses mentioned. He was an experienced Architectural Historian and was responsible for listing and assessing most of the listed buildings in the Parish. Section 15 keeps largely to the text and style of the original walk but with much additional material. The additions mostly come from Prebend. Bennet's unpublished " History of Pilton" [as indeed did most of the original Walks anecdotal information].This is available at S.R.O D\P\pilt/23/18. Prebend. Bennet was Vicar of Pilton from 1899 -1934 and collected information on Pilton over many years. This section also includes information provided by the late David Chapman.

2 Some of the details included in the original walk have been extended and moved to other sections of this History, and included below are some extracts from Parish registers given in the original "Walk" but not included elsewhere.

   1577   "There fell so great a snowe that no man could travel without danger of drowning therein."

   1580   "On Wednesdaye in the Easter weeke about 5 of the cloke in the afternoune there was a marvellous   earthquake most terrible and fearfull to the hartes of all men."

   1595   34 people were lost from the Plague.

   1701   About four o'clock "in ye afternoone" on Christmas Day, "william Warrin was killed by the falle of a pinnacle" from the south east corner of the church.

   1769   A large comet was seen in the "Est" for many days in September. The comet, discovered by French astromoner Messier, will not be seen again for a few thousand years.

   1860   Little John Corp, aged 7 ½, was mortally burned by a fire he kindled to warm himself in the field when he took food to his brother who was employed in "keeping birds".

   1877   Even smaller Helena Lawrence, aged 1, fell into the clothes washing pail and was "posened by the suds".

3. Cedar House information is from a letter by a relation of John Beale P.V.H.G L/006.

4. Little Malta information provided by David Chapman and Bob Hiscox.P.V.H.G. L/003.

5. Hartley house Bakery sold by Mr. Binnings in 1981 see P.V.H.G. D/001

6. Details of the 1893 Brewery sale are from P.V.H.G. D/001

7. The Smithy at Yew Tree Cottage is marked on the 1839 Tithe map.

8. First mention of a fair in Pilton that has been found is in Kellys Directory for 1861 but it is likely to have been an event for many years before this.It is also mentioned in a local history of Ditcheat that in 1877 a father kept his children off school as he needed the money to go to the Pilton Fair.

9. Pilton's listed buildings

The full details of each listed building can be found in S.R.O. DD\V/SMR/16(1-60)

Nos. 2, 3 Batch Cottages ,Bread St.
Malta House,Little Malta, Bread St.
Mulberry Cottage, Bread St.
Arch Villa, Bread St.
Tithe Barn, Cumhill
Manor House & Dovecote,Cumhill
St. Mary's Cottage, St. Mary's Lane
Monks Mill ,Shop Lane
Stone Cottage & Laurel Cottage ,Shop Lane
Church of St. John the Baptist ,Shop Lane
The Dell & Whiteleaf Cottage,Weir Lane
Yew Tree Cottage, Shutwell Lane
Wesley and Methodist Chapel, Top Street.
Corner Cottage & Clematis Cottage ,Whitestone Hill
Crown Inn, Whitestone Hill
Pilton Stores, Westholme Road
Durston Cottage & Toll cottage ,Park Hill
Orchard House, Pylle Rd.
Hazeldene & Benleigh Cottages, Pylle Road
Ebenezer Chapel, Pylle Rd.
Grey Gables , John Beale's Hill
Beales House, John Beales Hill
The Gable House, Lower Road
Pilton House, Lower Road.

Stable & Coach House adjacent to Pilton House
Yew Tree Farmhouse ,wall & Gate,Neat Lane
East Town Farmhouse, Easttown
Riverdale, East town
Wellands, East town
Springfield, Stable & Coach house, Neat Lane
Lamberts Hill Farmhouse, Lamberts Hill
Compton Court .East Compton
Compton House / Barn & coach house, East Compton
East Compton Farmhouse, East Compton
Manor Farmhouse, East Compton
Orchardleigh House, East Compton
Old Burford Farmhouse, Burford
Manor House,West Compton
West Compton House, West Compton
Knowle Farmhouse, West Compton
Red House Farmhouse, Worminster
Westholme House,Upper Westholme
Westholme Cottage, Perridge Hill
Higher Westholme Farmhouse, Perridge Hill
Perridge House, Perridge Hill
Hearne House, Lower Westholme Road
Holt Farmhouse, Holt Lane